IRAN AND THE BOMB

The CERI Series in Comparative Politics and International Studies

Series editor CHRISTOPHE JAFFRELOT

This series consists of translations of noteworthy publications in the social sciences emanating from the foremost French research centre in international studies, the Paris-based Centre d'Études et de Recherches Internationales (CERI), part of Sciences Po and associated with the CNRS (Centre National de la Recherche scientifique).

The focus of the series is the transformation of politics and society by transnational and domestic factors—globalisation, migration and the postbipolar balance of power on the one hand, and ethnicity and religion on the other. States are more permeable to external influence than ever before and this phenomenon is accelerating processes of social and political change the world over. In seeking to understand and interpret these transformations, this series gives priority to social trends from below as much as the interventions of state and non-state actors.

Founded in 1952, CERI has fifty full-time fellows drawn from different disciplines conducting research on comparative political analysis, international relations, regionalism, transnational flows, political sociology, political economy and on individual states.

Thérèse Delpech

Iran and the Bomb
The Abdication of International Responsibility

Translated by Ros Schwartz

Columbia University Press
New York

In association with the Centre d'Études et de Recherches Internationales, Paris

First published in 2006 by Éditions Autrement, Paris,
as *L'Iran, la bombe et la démission des nations*
© Éditions Autrement, 2006

Columbia University Press
Publishers Since 1893
New York

© Thérèse Delpech, 2007
English translation © CERI, Paris, 2006
Translated from the French by Ros Schwartz
All rights reserved

Library of Congress Cataloging-in-Publication Data

Delpech, Thérèse.
  [Iran, la bombe et la démission des nations. English]
  Iran and the bomb : the abdication of international responsibility /
Thérèse Delpech ; translated from the French By Ros Schwartz.
     p. cm.
  Includes bibliographical references and index.
  ISBN 978-0-231-70006-1 (cloth : alk. paper)
  1. Nuclear nonproliferation—Iran. 2. Iran—Foreign relations—
1997– 3. World politics—1989– I. Schwartz, Ros. II. Title.

JZ5665.D4513 2007
327.1'7470955—dc22

                                        2007020770
∞
Columbia University Press books are printed on permanent and durable acid-free paper.
This book is printed on paper with recycled content.
Printed in India

c 10 9 8 7 6 5 4 3 2 1

References to Internet Web sites (URLs) were accurate at the time of writing.
Neither the author nor Columbia University Press is responsible for URLs
that may have expired or changed since the manuscript was prepared.

CONTENTS

Acknowledgements

I should like to thank Christophe Jaffrelot and Henry Dougier for instigating this project, Michael Dwyer for his support and Ros Schwartz for the intelligence and dedication that she brought to the translation.

Paris, September, 2006   T.D.

Iran says the opposite of what it thinks and does the opposite of what it says, which does not necessarily mean that it does the opposite of what it thinks.

—A Western diplomat serving in Tehran

FOREWORD

Iran presents the international community with one of its greatest long-term challenges. The enormous area between Gaza and Afghanistan is vital to the future of international well-being. It spans the Middle East and the Persian Gulf, reaches in to Central and South Asia and holds energy resources on which much of the world's economic prospects hinge. It contains explosive conflicts between Israel and the Palestinians and their supporters; between the United States and the militants who want it to drive it from this part of the world; between Sunnis and Shiites; and between various autocracies and their frustrated citizens. Iran plays an increasingly central role in all of these conflicts and in the future of the entire region. It is the most populous country. Its overall energy resources are unsurpassed. Its population is the best educated and trained outside of Israel. Its civil society is the most vibrant, even as it faces increasing governmental repression. Iran's Revolutionary Guards and other clandestine actors also encourage and facilitate much of the violence and insecurity that others in the region fear.

If all of these concerns and issues were not enough, there is evidence that Iran is pursuing uranium enrichment and plutonium production capabilities that make sense only if Iranian leaders wish to be able to build nuclear weapons. If Iran's neighbors and other international players, including Israel and the United States, perceive that it has acquired a nuclear weapons capability, dangerous instability will follow. Some countries, perhaps including Egypt, Saudi Arabia and Turkey, will be tempted to match Iran at least by acquiring similar nuclear fuel production technologies. Some will be tempted to get tougher with Iran, and perhaps to strike militarily at it, unleashing a cycle of violent Iranian reaction. Some will be intimidated. A militant Iranian government that gains widespread popularity by threatening Israel and resisting the West may bolster the intensity and destructiveness of violent extremists in Lebanon, the Palestinian territories, Iraq, and elsewhere.

The implications of Iran's current and future policies, and the scope of its nuclear program, require exploration in a book, one that should also consider what has been and could be done to modify Iran's nuclear ambitions and make them more compatible with international peace and security. France, Germany, the United Kingdom, Russia, China, the European Union, the International Atomic Energy Agency, the United States and the UN Security Council all have been trying to alter Iran's behaviour—but we need Delpech's *Iran and the Bomb* to help explain what they have been doing and what still needs to be done.

Fortunately, Thérèse Delpech has produced such a book. This is fortunate not only because the subject matter is of vital importance, but also because she is an exceptionally well qualified author. She is highly informed about the Iranian nuclear program and the efforts to deal with it, as she has been involved with this challenge for more than a decade as a French government official. And she is a highly regarded strategist and historian of nuclear weapons, and hence can place the Iranian challenge in several contexts. Delpech is also an exceptionally lucid and trenchant writer: her recent book, *L'Ensauvagement*, won the Femina Prize, one of France's great literary awards, and will be published in English in early 2007 by the Carnegie Endowment for International Peace. With an author possessing these attributes, Delpech offers readers an outstandingly capable and enjoyable guide through a troubling subject. There is one more attribute that should be mentioned, too. Thérèse Delpech always displays the courage of her convictions. She neither avoids controversy nor dilutes her analysis and prose to suit the widest possible taste. Readers will not be bored.

George Perkovich
Washington, Carnegie Endowment for International Peace
October 2006

INTRODUCTION

The Islamic Republic of Iran is already twenty-eight years old. In appraising its evolution, the western world has continuously made serious errors of judgement, beginning by not foreseeing the advent of the 1979 Revolution. These errors have been repeated regularly because they reflect our wishes: we were lulled into believing in the triumph of reform over the revolutionary spirit, in the irresistible power of Iranian society's aspirations and in Tehran's reconciliation with the west. Some even contended that Iran had stopped supporting terrorism. And each time we were disillusioned. The shock at the outcome of the presidential elections in 2005 was particularly severe. Foreign diplomats serving in Tehran had all predicted the victory of Hashemi Rafsanjani. Governments believed the diplomats and set about preparing a far-reaching nuclear agreement deemed acceptable to all.[1] But the leader who emerged from the ballot like a rabbit from a magician's hat came from a very different background. Mahmoud Ahmadinejad, an ultra-conservative, former member of the Iranian secret service, member of the Pasdaran (Islamic Revolutionary Guards), was a hardliner. With him, there was no chance of a compromise. It became clear that sooner or later, it would be a question of bow or break. During the first six months, all concerned chose rather to bow.

There was hardly any excuse for this attitude, as, after the end of Khatami's presidency, alarm bells had soon begun to ring. Between the investiture of the new president on 1 August 2005 and the following December, the regime's stance both inside and outside the country hardened relentlessly: uranium conversion began again at Isfahan. "Martyrdom everywhere in the world" was hailed as "the greatest of acts" by the new president—a clear encouragement of terrorism. Lawyers like Abdolfatta Soltani, famous for defending opponents of the regime, were imprisoned, and Mahmoud Ahmadinejad described Israel as a "tumour that should be wiped off the map".

These words provoked public statements in the Western world and at the United Nations: many heads of state and political leaders described the Iranian president's comments about Israel as "unacceptable"; the Secretary General of the United Nations cancelled a trip to Tehran. But the main point appears not to have been understood: Mahmoud Ahmadinejad was not someone with whom it would be possible to negotiate. Furthermore, he had not been elected to negotiate. His mission was rather to lead Iran's nuclear weapons programme through its final stages.

That said, Western hopes were not entirely unfounded: young people in Iran have enormous expectations and are avid for change, and Iran is far from achieving its development potential. It has huge economic needs. One day, reality will perhaps prevail over rhetoric and ideology. *But Iran would still have the bomb.* For the time being, however, this populist and unscrupulous individual wilfully pursues his own agenda and aspires to lead the Muslim world, issuing radical statements. He may help strengthen Tehran's role in the Middle East by demonstrating its ability to stand up to "Western pressure" and condemn the State of Israel to the point of wanting to erase it from the map.

Iran's development is therefore dangerous: even the dramatic events in Lebanon in July 2006 may have their origin in Tehran—as an attempt to divert the international focus away from Iran's nuclear programme at a time when the United Nations Security Council (UNSC) was again addressing the issue. It is futile to count on in-fighting within the inner circle of power, even if there is a lively debate in Tehran on the most appropriate strategy. There has been no real internal conflict so far, probably because Iran has not yet paid any price for its audacious policy. In fact, Hashemi Rafsanjani, himself an advocate of opening up to the global economy, has been called on by the regime for tours of the Gulf. Since August 2005, he has made hardline speeches, unexpected from the lips of a man considered a moderate. Nor has Mahmoud Ahmadinejad miscalculated the effect of his tough stance, contrary to what some Iranian experts claim on the airwaves to comfort those who seek reassurance. His words are calculated: he expresses in a transparent way the very ideas not of the Iranian people but of the Iranian regime.

June 2005 was the beginning of a period of deliberate confrontation, which is not what was envisaged by the Europeans, the Americans or a large majority of Iranians themselves a year ago. This confrontation does not exclude discussion, according to a principle borrowed directly by Tehran from Mao Zedong which can be translated as "fight, fight, talk, talk". If Iran can combine the acquisition of the bomb and lengthy talks with the Europeans, Russians or Chinese with impunity on the international stage, this will naturally be its preferred option.

What this confrontation does rule out however is the possibility of reaching any agreement that would be acceptable to those who believe it is too risky to allow Iran to acquire the nuclear bomb, which would cause regional and global disruption. This camp has convincing arguments: an Iranian bomb would effectively strengthen the more radical elements in Iran who would be buoyed up by this success, and could result in a Middle East with a number of nuclear actors that would make it utterly unpredictable and even unmanageable. Saudi Arabia, Egypt, Syria and Turkey could leap into the breach and change their minds about not acquiring nuclear weapons. The Iranian bomb would thus jeopardise the fragile hopes of any virtuous circle in the region, and possibly—after North Korea's withdrawal from the Treaty on the Non-Proliferation of Nuclear Weapons in 1993—the entire non-proliferation regime, which would not be able to withstand an assault of this magnitude in a strategically sensitive part of the world.

Until now, the unacceptability of an Iranian nuclear bomb was—for the above reasons—the conviction of the Europeans and the Americans, and also of the Russians and a number of developing countries. Have they changed their views? No, they have not. They still think these dangers exist and could profoundly disrupt the international order for a long time. They still believe that their own security would be threatened as a result. But if that is the case, then why did the Permanent Five wait until February 2006 before they decided to inform the UN Security Council?[2] Why in March did they give the impression at the Security Council that they had opted for a long and slow strategy when the only way to make Tehran react would have been to take rapid measures that might prompt Ali Khamenei himself to reflect on the dangers of confrontation?[3] Why did the Europeans not recall their ambassadors in autumn 2005, rather than simply repeat that Mahmoud Ahmadinejad's comments on Israel were "unacceptable"? For a simple reason that history has seen time and time again: the western democracies seem unable to take action against an authoritarian regime that is bent on confrontation. They have difficulty in understanding that time is not on their side as a result of their sluggishness and their adversary's haste. By the time this glaring difference in pace emerges, it is usually too late.[4] The chances of stopping Iran in its race to acquire the nuclear bomb through diplomacy are therefore increasingly slender: too many opportunities have been missed and too much time lost. If the international community has proved powerless, each nation should acknowledge its responsibility: the Europeans have always reacted too little and too late, the Americans have not defined a clear policy on Iran, the Russians have constantly sat on the fence, and the Chinese have hidden behind the Russians. There will be a price to pay for tolerating the dubious role played by a country such as Pakistan, which only marginally assisted in the International Atomic Energy Agency (IAEA) investigation for fear that new evidence might come to light concerning its own proliferation activities, or South Africa, whose policy on Iran is hard to fathom. The aim of this book is to help clarify the role of these countries and many others in the drama that began in Iran over twenty years ago, in 1985, in the midst of the war against Iraq. It is necessary to go back that far, even if indications of this role only began to surface after the press conference held by the Iranian opposition in exile in August 2002.

The Iranian nuclear saga sheds an instructive light on international relations at the beginning of the twenty-first century, which are characterised by a failure of politics and by escalating violence. And as far as the Middle East is concerned, the fighting that broke out in July 2006 between Israel and Hizbullah highlighted dramatic changes in the region that go far beyond these events. It also proved a useful warning concerning both Iran's regional ambitions and what could be expected from Tehran *with* the bomb, taking into account what it already does *without* it.

IRAN: INDISPUTABLE MILITARY NUCLEAR AMBITIONS

2005 was a decisive year for Iran: the new president elected at the end of June marked a shift towards both increased internal authoritarianism and external provocation.[1] Worried by regional developments, and determined not to allow themselves to be caught out as in 1997, the Iranian authorities gave an additional turn of the screw. The January 2005 elections in Iraq showed that the Shia population could now freely choose its candidates, a worrying example for a neighbour battling for several years to re-establish an authoritarian stranglehold. Such a thing did not happen in Iran in the June presidential elections: the Pasdaran (around 150,000) and the Bassiji[2] (nearly a million) had received instructions from Ayatollah Khamenei. They were in charge of the organisation of the elections and they had considerable control over the way the ballots were counted.[3] Furthermore, the choice of a Kurdish Iraqi president in April also boded ill: around twenty Kurdish Iranian members of parliament then asked publicly why Iran needed to have a Shia president. The pluralist, federal and secular nature of the new Iraq, endorsed by the December 2005 elections, could only be a source of concern for the Iranian authorities. Lastly, Great Ayatollah Sistani had carefully distanced himself if not from politics, at least from wielding power in Iraq, which could be interpreted as a rejection of the system built by the mullahs in Iran.[4]

Syria's withdrawal from Lebanon in May 2005 was another blow, given Tehran's ties with Damascus, the defence agreement between the two countries and the way this withdrawal might modify the role of Hizbullah which had always benefited from Tehran's financial, military and political support.[5] The Lebanese elections in June, at the same time as the presidential election in Iran, confirmed the victory of Syria's opponents. Lastly, Ariel Sharon's determination to implement his plan to withdraw unilaterally from Gaza gained international support, including at the United Nations. Regional developments could therefore have driven the Ayatollah Ali Khamenei to opt for Ahmadinejad, who, apart from his loyalty and toughness, offered the advantage for the most deprived sectors of the population of not being corrupt, which could hardly be said of Hashemi Rafsanjani. This radical choice can be interpreted as a nervous reaction to a potentially threatening regional development. But it can also be seen as a challenge to the outside world, the new president being a man for whom compromise was not an option.

On top of internal and regional considerations, the international situation was then dominated by the nuclear case. It was becoming clear that it would be difficult for Iran to acquire a nuclear weapon and at the same time develop the country's economy. Particularly as there is no "eastern alternative" to Western investment in Iran, contrary to what Tehran would have us believe. What line was Iran to take? Agree to implement a purely civil nuclear energy programme and abandon the bomb, or count on a feeble reaction from the international community and collide head-on with it? The risk that Tehran would choose the latter, with the support of the "will of the people" and an authoritarian regime was greater than ever. Iran prepared public opinion for confrontation, disdaining those opposed to its nuclear ambitions, from whom it thinks it has little to fear. The demonstrations outside the British and French embassies in Tehran in 2005, the attempts to intimidate European diplomats in Iran and the violence over the cartoons of the Prophet, just when it was decided to refer the Iranian case to the Security Council, sent out a clear signal to this effect.

But to grasp the nature of this crisis, it is essential to have a sound understanding both of what the Iranian government *wants* to achieve through its nuclear programme, and secondly of what it *can* achieve, both politically and technically. There are different answers to the first question:

1. *Iran wants to develop its own nuclear fuel cycle for civilian purposes.* This is what Tehran has continually claimed, and has maintained since the election of the new president: the programme is entirely peaceful and there is no reason to deprive Iran of its "inalienable" right to benefit from nuclear energy for peaceful purposes guaranteed by article 4 of the Treaty on the Non-Proliferation of Nuclear Weapons (NPT). It is Iran's chief propaganda argument. The problem with this argument is not only that it is an abusive interpretation of the NPT, which guarantees neither enrichment nor reprocessing, but only the right to use nuclear energy for "peaceful purposes". These needs can be fulfilled by outside supplies (as is the case for example of South Korea, Finland and Sweden which have a much bigger nuclear power capacity.[6] Furthermore, this right is dependent on countries fulfilling their non-proliferation obligations. The main issue is not that Iran's abundant oil and gas resources are so massive that developing nuclear energy does not make much sense from an economic point of view.[7] After all Iran is entitled to seek to diversify its energy resources which is purely a matter for it to decide. The problem lies elsewhere: first of all, this "peaceful" programme was shrouded in great secrecy for nearly twenty years (1985-2002), and was only disclosed by the Iranian opposition in exile. Moreover, there is no economic rationale for Iran's fuel cycle ambitions given that for the single Russian-built reactor under construction, agreements were signed with Russia in 2005 guaranteeing its operation for more than ten years. In fact, there is a general agreement for its entire lifetime, which is around thirty

years.[8] Lastly, the international inspectors identified nuclear activities on military-controlled sites which could be compatible with a nuclear power programme (enrichment in Brazil is controlled by the navy, and components for centrifuges can be manufactured in the military work-shops which also produce components for missiles using the same type of equipment), but when the inspectors are not granted access to the sites in question, or access is delayed, or even major demolition works are carried out before the inspection date, it is reasonable to question the purpose of the activities being conducted on these sites.[9]

Iran's decision to build 54,000 centrifuges in Natanz,[10] to develop a laser enrichment programme at Lashkar Abad[11] and to build a heavy-water reactor at Arak, which is still under construction,[12] is incon-sistent with the presence of a single Russian-built reactor on Iranian soil, which can only operate with Russian fuel. On a more detailed examination of this programme, it quickly became apparent that the decision to resume nuclear activities was taken in 1985, in the middle of the war against Iraq, at a time when there was no reactor to justify it but the nation was under threat.[13] Secondly, the performance of the centrifuges at Natanz is not very high, whereas in 1995, Iran acquired a blueprint for a much more efficient machine from Pakistan's clandes-tine Abdul Qadeer Khan network,[14] and it is still not known what Iran did with it between 1995 and 2002. But in May 2004, Iran acknowl-edged that it had purchased magnets for these centrifuges from Asian suppliers. Thirdly, laser enrichment for civil nuclear power generation purposes consumes more electricity than it produces and there is no real rationale for it other than the production of small quantities of ma-terials as part of a weapons programme. In addition, laser equipment at Lashkar Abad was dismantled and moved elsewhere before Iran al-lowed the IAEA to inspect in August 2003.[15] Finally, the heavy-water reactors produce large amounts of plutonium and are therefore very useful if Iran pursues the plutonium route to make the bomb.[16] If Iran wants nuclear technology purely for civil power generation purposes, why was it in such a hurry to resume uranium conversion activities in August 2005, in the absence of any industrial requirements? Why did it refuse to examine the European proposal to replace this type of reactor by a proliferation-resistant pressurised water reactor? Why too did it refuse on several occasions to take advantage of enrichment services provided by Europe and Russia? And lastly, why can such a large proportion of Iran's imports or attempted imports during the entire period 1985-2002—and beyond—not be counted as part of its civil nuclear energy programme?

That said, if Iran wanted to develop a nuclear energy programme, the Europeans never tried to prevent it. The offer they made in August 2005 provided guarantees of additional fuel supplies in the event of the Russian supply failing. It also included giving Iran access to markets for reactors designed to produce nuclear energy. And the offer of June 2006 made by the five permanent members of the Security Council and Germany was even more enticing. After having aroused so much understandable suspicion as to its real intentions, Tehran's only solution, if reason were to prevail, would be to agree to cease all enrichment and reprocessing activities in exchange for guarantees from Russia and Europe that the necessary fuel for its reactor—and later possibly for its many reactors—would regularly be supplied by third-party countries. Russia asked no more than to be that supplier, which would guarantee lucrative foreign currency contracts for Moscow. For the region and for the world, it is a question of vital trust-building measures.

2. *Iran wants to use its nuclear programme as a bargaining tool with the Americans.* This argument has often been applied to North Korea: Pyongyang is supposedly developing its nuclear activities with the aim of entering into negotiations with Washington. If sufficiently attractive conditions could be agreed, then Kim Il-sung's nuclear ambitions and, since 1994, those of Kim Jong-il, would be curbed. This hypothesis is hardly borne out by events, for the fact is that North Korea, home to one of the most brutal dictatorships ever known, wants to acquire the nuclear bomb to guarantee the regime's survival. Even after

Pyongyang's declarations that it had nuclear weapons and wanted the moratorium on ballistic missile testing to be lifted, there were some who still advocated entering into a bilateral dialogue to strike a "global deal" without realising that this was impossible with Pyongyang.[17] This approach, already attempted in 1993-1994, had culminated in an agreement in October 1994 that foundered in autumn 2002 when North Korea rejected it and then withdrew from the NPT in January 2003. Two and a half years later, the joint declaration of September 2005—promising dismantlement of the nuclear programme—once again gave rise to false hopes which were soon dashed by events.

In Iran's case, there might have been a chance, at least before the presidential elections, of renewing contact with Washington after relations were severed at the time of the hostage crisis, in 1979, the year of the Islamic revolution. Iran would have had good reasons to try and seek security guarantees from Washington, which named Iran as one of the countries belonging to the "axis of evil" and talked from time to time of a "regime change" in Tehran. Iraq's experience in particular showed how quickly the US troops were able to defeat Saddam Hussein in April 2003, even if they have since encountered unforeseen difficulties. Furthermore, Iran needs American and European investment to optimise its gas and petroleum industry. Western investment is unthinkable unless the question of Iran's unconventional weapons programme is resolved, as the example of Libya has already demonstrated. Iran could therefore legitimately have sought a dialogue with Washington and tried to do so from a position of strength. The Europeans would then only have served to curry favour with the USA. This scenario was perhaps intellectually plausible until June 2005. As a matter of fact, it was above all between 1997 and 1999, when President Khatami still enjoyed the support of the Iranian people and particular that of the youth population, that an American initiative could have been successful. But in choosing as president a man as radical as Mahmoud Ahmadinejad, Tehran cannot still expect to achieve this outcome, since it consciously chose adversarial relations with the West.

Moreover, these purported intentions would not explain a programme launched twenty years ago, in the middle of the war against Iraq! At the time, the war against Iraq was Iran's biggest problem, especially as two years earlier Saddam Hussein had taken the decision to use chemical weapons against the Iranian troops. The question that preoccupied Tehran was not only the entire Western world's support for Baghdad, but also its unacceptable silence on Iraq's use of weapons prohibited by the 1925 Geneva Protocol banning the use of biological and chemical weapons. All the Western countries were signatories, and some—like France—were even depositaries.

The fact that Iran's nuclear programme was clearly not conceived as a bargaining tool does not mean that it could not ever become one. If the Europeans had not believed it possible, they would not made two attempts, on 21 October 2003 and 15 November 2004, to seek a negotiated solution with Tehran, proposing on each occasion the suspension of nuclear fuel cycle activities, with a view to discontinuing them. However they were always conscious that this was a risky gamble with a slim chance of success, and that Washington rather than London, Paris or Berlin held the trump cards, both economic and strategic.

But in summer 2006, all this is history. After Iran violated the second agreement in August 2005, resumed enrichment activities in January 2006 and categorically refused to bow to the demands of the IAEA Board of governors and UN Security Council, the idea of a third round of negotiations reflected the triumph of hope over experience, as the fate of the P6 offer demonstrated in summer 2006.[18]

3. *Iran simply wants the bomb*. By the 1990s, this was already the conclusion of a number of observers of Iran's ballistic missile programme, whose scope and configurations are compatible with a nuclear weapons programme. At this point, all the indicators corroborate this hypothesis. For although there were significant agreements between Iran and Europe (October 2003, then November 2004), followed by thorough international inspections, this is indisputably what is known about Iran's nuclear programme. The IAEA had already gathered a body of

evidence against Iran in 2003, but the discoveries of the last three years are of capital importance, be it Tehran's acquisition of blueprints for second-generation or P2 centrifuges, nuclear activities conducted on the military site of Lavizan, which still remain unexplained, the existence of a nuclear offer from Pakistan back in 1987, the exact nature of which is unknown, experiments conducted with plutonium or Iran's possession of the technology for producing and casting uranium metal into hemispheres which have solely military applications, and which constitutes a direct violation of article 2 of the NPT.

Iran's initial explanations regarding many points have had to be modified in the light of the inspectors' discoveries and revelations from outside. The extensive data from the investigation that followed Colonel Gaddafi's disclosures about his own programme at the end of 2003 and the discovery of the clandestine Pakistani network are good examples. A member of the network, B.S. Tahir, questioned in Malaysia, admitted to having sold to Iran in 1994 blueprints for centrifuges that were much more sophisticated than those which Iran had so far admitted to owning.[19] Tehran was forced to rectify its declarations on this subject in March 2004. The history as well as the whereabouts of these P2 machines is still unknown. The answer is likely to be found on military sites—under the authority of the Revolutionary Guards—to which the inspectors have not yet been granted access, or to which they have had only partial or delayed access.

The IAEA reports show that the inspectors did not waste their time however, even though they did not always take full advantage of the powers conferred on them. Although the hundreds of inspections on Iranian soil left them with significant uncertainties, their observations still go far beyond what Iran was prepared to admit to at the beginning of the investigation. The list of violations committed by Iran grows ever longer: in 2005 for example, the inspectors discovered tunnels excavated near the Isfahan conversion facility—the blueprint for which Iran should have handed over to the IAEA—built to store nuclear materials produced at the plant. They also made a more significant discovery: that of a nuclear offer from Pakistan dated 1987, the original of which was presented to the inspectors in an incomplete form.[20] No copy of the offer that would permit the inspectors either to identify its author or to discover its exact content was ever produced.[21] Crucially, they finally acquired the proof that uranium metal producing and casting technology had been supplied to Tehran. The 1987 Pakistani offer might even have included, as in the case of Libya, a weapon design.[22] To sum up, the quest for an atomic weapon is the only credible explanation for the secrecy that surrounded the programme, the involvement of the military, the multiple purchases and attempted purchases traced around the world,[23] and Iran's many lies, ploys and stalling tactics.

4. *What are Iran's technical capabilities?* It is very difficult to answer this question for one simple reason: even if a great deal of important data has been gathered since February 2003, the full extent of the programme is still not known. It is for such reasons that the IAEA report of 3 September 2005 requests extended powers to pursue its investigation. Most observers are in agreement that some sites, activities, and even materials may have escaped detection by the inspectors and intelligence services. Iran has indeed demonstrated its ability to conceal large nuclear facilities for a long time. By definition, the state of progress of activities on these sites is unknown, even if there is speculation on the subject. It could be a matter of clandestine uranium enrichment activities and experiments directly linked to the development of the nuclear bomb.

Furthermore, a number of known sites controlled either by the military or the Pasdaran are either not accessible, or only partially accessible to international inspections. This applies to the Lavizan-Shian site, where six buildings were demolished before the arrival of the inspectors in April 2004. It is still true of the Parchin site, dedicated to missiles and activities associated with high-intensity explosives. Explosives testing could have taken place there, as well as laser enrichment. A very incomplete inspection was carried out on 12 January 2005, and the second inspection, authorised much later in the year, proved fruitless: Iran had had ample time to conceal anything it wanted to hide. And last but not least, Iran has considerably restricted access to its known nuclear facilities since February 2006.

There is speculation about the extent to which the programme "suspended" until August 2005 following agreements with Europe was necessary to the nuclear weapons programme. The conversion activities at Isfahan are probably necessary to this programme, given Iran's determination to resume them at all costs in August 2005, when there was no justification for a civil nuclear energy programme. But it cannot be ruled out that major progress was also made in other areas while the negotiations were ongoing—efficiency of centrifuges, for example, hexafluoride purification, or more direct weapons-related activities, as Hassan Rohani[24] claims in his "testament" of July 2005.

Given the abrupt way in which the Iranian opposition divulged information on Iran's activities in 2002, it is also likely that the sites of Natanz, Arak, Lashkar Abad and Isfahan were part of the nuclear weapons programme and that the production of the necessary fissile materials relied, at least in part, on having access to known uranium conversion and enrichment facilities. In any case, Iran has so far acquired the capability to convert uranium concentrate to uranium tetrafluoride (UF_4), and then to convert uranium tetrafluoride to uranium hexafluoride (UF_6) or uranium metal, as well as subsequent enrichment to produce weapon-grade uranium. In 2006, Iran is on the verge of mastering critical steps in building and operating a gas centrifuge plant.

This does not automatically mean that Iran has overcome all the technical obstacles. It is not certain what advances have been made since 2003. Trials without nuclear materials might have been carried out to test the other parts of the nuclear warhead. Iran has mastered ballistic missile technology and has learned a great deal about it from North Korea and most probably Russia as well. Improvements have been made to the Shehab 3 missile which may well now have a range of

1200 miles, and there are reports that Iran bought 18 BM-25 missiles from North Korea. This is a nuclear missile which is more sophisticated than the Shehab-3.

Here again, Pakistani and North Korean partnerships may have been very helpful to Iran, but still in 2006 observers are unclear about the extent of its relations with these two countries. Supplies from Pakistan may have been more extensive and more diverse than is admitted publicly, and it is not in Islamabad's interest to give too detailed information on its past collaborations. This particularly as Islamabad may be under pressure from Beijing which might find itself implicated once more in a serious case of nuclear proliferation (as it already has been in Libya: the weapon design supplied to Tripoli by Pakistan was of Chinese origin). As for North Korea, whose partnership with Iran over ballistic missiles is well documented, it is not impossible that it has also collaborated with Tehran on some joint nuclear activities, as Japanese sources regularly claim. If a North Korean nuclear test were to take place one day, as is announced from time to time, it would make sense to ask whether Tehran might not be the second beneficiary of the test results.[25]

To conclude the question of Iran's technical advances, let us cite the words of Mullah Hassan Rohani on 23 July 2005, mentioned earlier. The Secretary of the Supreme National Security Council and lead negotiator with the Europeans effectively declared that "astonishing results have been achieved on the technical front". This may have been propaganda, but we cannot discount the fact that as another negotiator, Sirus Nasseri, had already asserted in December 2004 for Iran, as with North Korea, the main purpose of the diplomatic exercise was to allow it to pursue its clandestine activities unimpeded.[26] Nor is it impossible that the number of available centrifuges is greater than thought,[27] that the quantity of UF_6 produced is more than 110 metric tonnes, while the quality is purer,[28] and that the development of missiles to carry nuclear warheads is more advanced than was imagined.[29] There are simply too many unknowns to be able to make accurate calculations. But since the speed at which Iran is pursuing a nuclear capability is highly relevant, it appears that the minimum time needed for Iran to acquire enough nuclear material for a nuclear device is most probably about two years from now.

5. *What can Iran gain politically?* Iran's political game is transparent. A first objective is to guarantee the support of the non-aligned countries by insisting on the "inalienable" right of the signatories of the NPT to benefit from nuclear energy for peaceful purposes. According to the terms used by President Khatami during his trip to France at the beginning of April 2005, "giving up nuclear energy for peaceful purposes would be unacceptable".[30] This argument is repeated again and again in different guises. Tehran naturally neglects to mention that this right is linked to compliance with articles 1 and 2 of the NPT, stipulating the non-diversion of nuclear activities for military purposes. It neglects also to mention that the right to use nuclear energy for peaceful purposes can be fulfilled without enrichment or reprocessing taking place within the country concerned. And lastly it avoids responding to one of Europe's principal arguments, which is that there is no economic justification for fuel cycle activities given Iran's current energy and industrial circumstances.

But most of the political and diplomatic elites are ill-acquainted with these factors. Iran's insistence on the "right" to use nuclear energy for peaceful purposes is a winning ploy in a general climate where there is strong support for the theory that the northern countries have chosen to develop nuclear technology to maintain their domination over the south. Still, this rhetoric has its limits as some Arab Gulf states—Saudi Arabia first and foremost—do not want Iran to have a nuclear bomb and are not afraid to say so. Another leading Muslim country in the Middle East, Turkey, has expressed similar fears on several occasions. As regards India, a skilful advocate of developing countries' rights to modern technologies, it will not allow its situation to be compared to that of Iran, and twice passed resolutions—in September 2005 and in February 2006—against Tehran. This shows the limitations of the solidarity between some of the major players in the group of non-aligned countries, especially if we add that Brazil too voted in favour of referring Iran to the Security Council.

The second prong of Iran's political strategy consists of neutralising the Arab countries, which also fear an Iranian nuclear bomb, by continually evoking the Israeli nuclear threat and reinforcing the Arab populations' hostility towards Israel.[31] The Israeli nuclear threat is a forceful argument in the Arab world, even in moderate countries like Jordan and Egypt. Cairo has been playing an ambiguous game vis-à-vis Iran with its systematic obstruction at the NPT conference in May 2005, an attitude which clearly served Iran's interests.[32] The Arab countries consider tolerance of Israel's nuclear capability unacceptable. The argument that Israel has not signed the NPT and is not violating any international commitment in developing a nuclear capability, unlike Iraq in the past or Iran over the last two decades, is not accepted, even if it is legally valid.

The third prong of Iran's political strategy consists of challenging information on its nuclear programme by recalling the errors of judgement concerning Iraq's supposed weapons of mass destruction. Even if the information available on Tehran's activities chiefly comes not from the intelligence services or from Washington, but from the IAEA and external sources like members of Abdul Qadeer Khan's Pakistani network, the argument has a certain influence among those who have only a very general level of information on the Iranian case. One of the main differences between Iraq and Iran when it comes to sources of information is that in Iraq in the years prior to the intervention by the US and British troops in March 2003, Saddam Hussein's opponents passed on information that was uncorroborated or utterly false, whereas since 2002, the Iranian opposition has handed over extremely precise data, often confirmed by international inspections, which remains the principal source of information. This applied notably to the first sites of Natanz and Arak (enrichment and a reactor able to produce plutonium), then to the Kalaye Electric plant (pilot facility for centrifuge enrichment), and also to the site of Lashkar Abad (laser enrichment).

A fourth prong of Iran's strategy consists of constantly adapting to events by modifying previous declarations according to the inspectors' discoveries. For example, Tehran initially stated that the entire programme was to produce nuclear energy for domestic purposes. Then, when the inspectors found traces of high-enriched uranium, this declaration became dangerous because it proved that undeclared activities potentially contrary to the NPT had been carried out on Iranian soil. Since then, Iran has explained these traces as resulting from contamination by imported centrifuge components (probably from Pakistan). And contamination by low-enriched and high-enriched uranium is still one of the main unresolved questions for the international inspectors in August 2006. In fact, China, Russia and Pakistan have all supplied Iran with major elements for its nuclear programme, which is anything but a civilian nuclear programme.

The final prong of Iran's strategy consists of dividing the various players involved. In autumn 2002, after a press conference called by the Iranian opposition in exile, it was chiefly the IAEA that was negotiating with Iran. This first stage was difficult for Tehran and the resolution adopted by the Agency's Council of Governors in Vienna in September 2002 was followed by a five-month delay—between October 2002 and February 2003—before Iran would admit the international inspectors.[33] During this period, the Tehran authorities had to adjust to the situation created by the disclosures and make accommodations, which probably entailed relocating equipment and documents. Once the inspections began, these only confirmed the opposition's revelations, in more specific detail, reinforcing their seriousness.[34] This led to a new resolution being adopted by the IAEA Board of Governors, in September 2003, giving Tehran an ultimatum. It was at this stage that the Europeans entered the arena to try and broker a negotiated solution without taking the case to the UN Security Council. It has since become clear that the suspension of the referral of Iran's case to the Security Council and the suspension of Iranian fuel cycle activities go hand in hand. If the latter is in doubt, as it was in August 2005, then the former should be halted. This explains President Chirac's declaration at the end of August 2005 during the Conference of Ambassadors, indicating that the Europeans would have no choice but to refer the case to the United Nations Security Council. It is hard to understand why such a clear intention was not put into immediate effect in September, or only deferred until November 2005. When action was finally envisaged in February 2006, after more than five months during which Iran had been quietly able to pursue its conversion activities at Isfahan and resume its enrichment activities at Natanz, it was still a matter of merely informing the Security Council, which precluded any decision being taken before March. This was despite the lack of any breakthroughs in the "negotiations" with Russia, and with Tehran announcing on 13 February that discussions with the Russians, initially scheduled for the 16 of that month were adjourned indefinitely.[35] Later, during 2006, the same diplomatic sluggishness continued to prevail, to the extent that Resolution 1696 making suspension compulsory (see Appendix 4) was only adopted at the end of July, five months after Iran was referred to the Security Council.

Iran's 2003 and 2004 agreements with the Europeans were never implemented in good faith and one may even wonder whether Tehran has ever negotiated at all. Iran seems rather to have seized on these proposals as giving extra room and time for manoeuvre. In 2003, no sooner had the demands of Paris, Berlin and London been accepted, than they were criticised in Tehran[36] for going beyond the demands of the IAEA statute, and confusion soon set in too concerning the question of the precise scope of the activities suspended according to the Agreement of 21 October, which refers only to uranium enrichment without specifying any further.

Iran's efforts to create a rift between the Europeans and the IAEA met with a degree of success, but failed when Tehran attempted to split the Europeans. They succeeded in maintaining a united front during the two rounds of negotiations conducted with Iran.[37] Then Tehran tried to drive a wedge between the Europeans and the Russians, at the time contracted to supply fuel to the Bushehr plant. Once again, they failed, even if Moscow's policy lacked transparency, and still does. The Europeans were careful to maintain regular and detailed information channels with Moscow. They eventually convinced the Russians that they were not seeking to compete with them commercially and that the ongoing negotiations with Iran were not jeopardised by the Russian contract to supply fuel to Bushehr. The contract showed, on the contrary, the futility of Iran embarking on a complete fuel production cycle.

Lastly, transatlantic relations were a delicate matter because of the wounds left by the invasion of Iraq. Iran thought it would be easy to divide the Europeans and the Americans, despite the presence of the British in the European troika. But Jack Straw, the Foreign Secretary, was one of the most enthusiastic supporters of a negotiated solution with Tehran, whereas from 2003, the USA had been pushing to report Iran to the Security Council. Iran sought to obtain from the Europeans a promise to withdraw Iran's case from the agenda of the IAEA Board of Governors,[38] and then not to refer it to the Security Council or subject it to sanctions, and that they would oppose any use of force and finally refuse to take part if any such action were to be envisaged by the USA. On all these points, the Europeans would have found themselves in direct conflict with Washington. It is not certain whether Tehran believed that the European capitals could make such pledges or whether the Iranian authorities reckoned they had nothing to lose in trying this tactic. However, there too things did not go the way Tehran had hoped and instead transatlantic relations have improved since the beginning of the Iran crisis. This is particularly true since President Bush's visit to Europe at the beginning of 2005,[39] during which it was decided that the USA would take a softer line,[40] while the Europeans would make a firmer commitment in the event of a breach of the Paris Agreement or new violations discovered by the IAEA. Even in autumn 2005, while the weaknesses of the European strategy were becoming increasingly apparent, it is remarkable that Washington showed no impatience.

A political victory was however won by Tehran at the 2005 Review Conference of the Parties to the Treaty on the Non-Proliferation of Nuclear Weapons. Tehran effectively obstructed the agenda for more than a week—with the unexpected help of Egypt—claiming that the events that had occurred between 2000 and 2005 should not be reviewed. The argument is all the more surprising given that the aim of these conferences is precisely to review the implementation of the Treaty every five years. But it was during this period that Iran's two decades of clandestine activities had come to light. Tehran was therefore trying to protect itself from references being made to the many violations identified in the IAEA's November 2004 report (and therefore undeniable in the eyes of the international community). Furthermore, by putting pressure on Russia, Iran managed to prevent the Conference from adopting a declaration by the five nuclear powers denouncing Iran's lies, its hindrance of the inspections and stalling tactics, which could have resulted in an agreement with the Security Council, of which these countries are permanent members. Finally, the Iranian delegation spoke last at this Conference, which ended without making the slightest progress.

The most recent political chapter opened after the 2005 presidential elections. An interview with Mullah Rohani published on 23 July 2005 states that from the beginning of the negotiations, it had been decided at the highest state level to consider the development of the fuel cycle in Iran as a "red line" on which there can be no compromise. He also emphasises that Tehran must retain control of the suspension of activities outlined in the agreements with the Europeans. He confirms that Iran's fear of being reported to the Security Council is real, particularly for economic reasons (fall in foreign investment), and that Tehran wants an end to the negotiations (less than a year) so that Iran can resume conversion and enrichment activities. It is clearly apparent from this interview that the main purpose of the discussions with the Europeans was to delay the prospect of referral to the Security Council. It also shows that the Europeans have been manipulated from the outset by Iran.[41] It finally reveals that Iran was more assiduous in achieving its objectives than those who were trying to prevent it. From the moment in January 2006 when discussions with the Europeans were officially broken off, Iran tried to repeat the same tactic with Moscow. And in summer 2006, Iran continues to do its utmost to gain time, so as to reach the point when the entire world will be confronted with the *fait accompli* of an uncontrollable process that will result in a nuclear bomb.[42] However, with the adoption of Resolution 1696 by the Security Council on 31 July, things may speed up. This Resolution effectively makes compulsory the suspension that Tehran has so far refused to implement.

2

EUROPE: AN INCREASINGLY
CONTROVERSIAL STRATEGY

Three years ago, the Europeans leapt into diplomatic action over Iran with the very best intentions. But now, in 2006, it is time to take stock of this action. To cut a very long story short, the foreign ministers of France, Britain and Germany had high expectations when they visited Tehran in October 2003, but these were not fulfilled. On the contrary, the negotiations may have been used by Tehran to gain precious time.

The whole saga started much earlier. Without going back to the time of the Shah, when Iran already had nuclear aspirations, some European countries have suspected it of having nuclear ambitions for a number of years, especially Germany, which was involved in the construction of the Bushehr power station before it was bombed by Iraq in 1983. This operation, justified at the time by the state of war between Iran and Iraq, was a replay of the destruction by the Israeli air force in 1981 of the 40-megawatt light-water Osirak nuclear reactor which France had unwisely sold to Baghdad. But the Iraqi operation on Bushehr did not come in for the same level of criticism given the interplay of alliances and support at the time. Once the war against Saddam Hussein was over, Tehran immediately asked the Germans to rebuild the plant, but prudently they refused on the grounds of regional tensions and the lack of any economic justification. France too refused, for the same reasons. In the late 1980s, Tehran, which had ploughed one billion dollars into the construction of the EURODIF enrichment facility in the south of France, sought to obtain low-enriched uranium by using this investment as a bargaining tool. But Paris stood firm: in the absence of any nuclear energy programme in Iran, there was no basis for selling it low-enriched uranium. Furthermore, since the bombing of the Osirak reactor, France had adopted a cautious policy of placing an embargo on the sale of any equipment or nuclear materials to the Middle East, for whatever stated or presumed purpose.

Since the end of the 1980s, Tehran's relentless determination to obtain nuclear equipment and materials from around the world has intrigued more than one European capital. Particularly as the country had such extensive oil and gas reserves, there was no justification for the rush to develop alternative energy sources. Iran's energy needs were not under threat, even in the long term, and Tehran even had a significant energy export policy, supplying energy to countries like China, India, Pakistan and South Africa. Why then such insistence on acquiring a nuclear capability? In the face of Europe's reluctance, Tehran turned to Moscow, which lent a more sympathetic ear, and signed a contract commissioning Russia to rebuild the Bushehr reactor in 1995. Then in 2005, Iran signed another deal with Russia to supply fuel for this reactor.

From the mid-1990s, the Europeans were aware of the possibility that this civil nuclear energy programme might enable Iran to obtain expertise and technology from the Russians other than those necessary for purely peaceful purposes.

And yet, for around a decade, the Europeans opted for "constructive dialogue" with Iran, while the USA continued to impose heavy sanctions, the roots of which were political, not only nuclear, as they went back to 1995, in response to Iran's support of terrorists *and* pursuit of nuclear technology. This lasted until the suspicions were confirmed by specific intelligence on Iranian acquisitions—sometimes from Europe—which could not be justified by a civil nuclear energy programme. From then on, Europe became more vigilant, particularly in controlling exports, and Iran's activities came under routine surveillance. Suspicions were confirmed by the disclosures of mid-2002, and the European troika quickly rallied to try and deal with the Iranian problem using the tool of diplomacy.

Originally the Europeans became involved in the Iranian case for three main reasons: they wanted to demonstrate that it was possible to achieve progress on non-proliferation by going down the diplomatic route; they sought to restore the unity they had lost during the Iraq crisis; and they themselves felt threatened by Iran's ballistic missile programme, given its existing and planned capability.

1. *Effective multilateralism* is what the Europeans would like to succeed when it comes to formulating their security policy, particularly over the question of the proliferation of non-conventional weapons. In June 2003, the European Union published a joint strategy for combating the proliferation of weapons of mass destruction (WMD). This document covers nuclear, biological and chemical weapons as well as their delivery systems (ballistic or cruise missiles). One of its main objectives was to show that multilateralism is not merely a way of delaying action, nor even the crises, as Washington often tends to believe, but a means of obtaining substantial results. The leading role played by the UK, Germany and France on the Iran question was supposed to illustrate this policy.

Another aspect of "effective multilateralism" appears in the Proliferation Security Initiative (PSI) launched in Krakow and signed in Paris in 2003. Its aim was to intercept planes, ships or ground transportation containing equipment and/or technologies destined for countries with clandestine WMD programmes. This initiative led to the interception, off the coast of Sicily in October 2003, of the German ship *BBC China*, which was transporting centrifuge parts to Libya. Further to revelations from Libya a few months later, the existence of a deal between the Pakistani network and Libya for L2-type centrifuges came to light. With both diplomatic negotiations and the possible interception of vessels transporting goods likely to be used in non-conventional weapons programmes, the expectation was to show that non-proliferation could work without resorting to the use of force.

The success or failure of negotiations with Iran will therefore certainly be interpreted in the broader context of European security policy. This policy is not confined to diplomacy. The Europeans had made it clear to Tehran that any violation of the 2003 and 2004 Agreements would result in Iran being reported to the Security Council, from which it had been shielded only because of Iran's decision to suspend its fuel cycle activities. In the event of violation, theoretically no type of action was excluded, not even the use of force as a last resort. But these threats were not implemented when Iran unilaterally twice broke the commitments made to the European capitals.

The Europeans' preference was clearly to convince Tehran to suspend the offending activities permanently without having to involve the Security Council, resort to sanctions or—even worse—to force. But this goal could never be achieved, Iran having repeated on numerous occasions that the Europeans' demands were unacceptable. The negotiations were broken off by Tehran in June 2004 and August 2005, placing the Europeans up against the wall, which is where they have been ever since.

2. *The solidarity of the three European countries.* For three years, despite their different approaches, London, Paris and Berlin have remained remarkably united over the Iran question, which has allowed the European Union as a whole to adopt the troika's positions. This unity, which was strengthened even further with the arrival of Germany's new chancellor, never allowed Tehran a chance to play off one capital against another or to obtain from one what had been refused by another. The British however have imperatives in Iraq which they must take into account, as Iran is capable of causing disruption in the majority Shia-controlled region of southern Iraq. Tehran agents have infiltrated this area, as "observers" since 2003, but they can switch to other types

of action if necessary, as they have made clear and even sometimes already demonstrated.[1] Paris and Berlin, while mindful of this concern, do not share it as they do not have troops in Iraq.

Joschka Fischer, the German foreign minister until autumn 2005 and leader of the Green party, had to take into account his party's anti-nuclear position and its hostility to the use of force under any circumstances. Despite a shift in opinion in Germany after the Balkan tragedy, there is still a strong opposition to the use of force, even in the event of blatant violation of international agreements, and the prospect of intervention is very unpopular in the whole country, not just among the Greens. Chancellor Schröder even tried, albeit unsuccessfully, to play this card in August 2005 during the electoral campaign.

As for France, its policy is often defined in opposition to that of Washington, and that is still a factor which Iran sometimes thinks it can manipulate. However, the three European countries' determination to stop what they see as a major threat to regional stability and an attack on the nuclear Non-Proliferation Treaty overrode these differences. They have defined their position in the event of a breakdown in the diplomatic process, and also made commitments to Washington should the negotiations founder. In July 2006, they all agreed on adopting UN Security Council resolution 1696 presenting Iran with an ultimatum. What will follow in the event that Iran does not comply is less clear.

3. *The Iranian threat seen from Europe.* Most observers interpreted the European initiative as a means of preventing an American intervention against Iran, particularly as it began in autumn 2003, just a few months after the US intervention in Iraq. But this interpretation is partial and does not take into account a central factor: the perception of an Iranian threat. True, the appearance of an Iranian nuclear bomb would first of all be a threat to the Middle East. It would give a boost to the most conservative elements in Tehran and help radicalise the fears of regional domination by Iran. As a result, it could also justify the development of new nuclear programmes. A Middle East with

multiple nuclear actors would be utterly impossible to control and altogether unpredictable. But Europe's interests are just as evident. Europe would like to play a greater political role in this region, while continuing directly to look after its own security interests—which could increase further if Turkey joins the EU within the next ten years. Europe's eastern frontier would then be in the heart of the Middle East, significantly altering the present situation. The Middle East's problems would truly become Europe's problems. European responsibilities for the region's stability would grow considerably, and Europe should also ensure that the Middle East does not export instability to its territory.

There is an even more direct threat, and that is the range of Iranian missiles. They can already reach European territory. It can be argued that Iran has no intention of attacking Europe. But, as during the Cold War, operational capabilities need to be taken into account rather than intentions; those can fluctuate and are, furthermore, often unknown. When Tehran tested its Shehab 3 missile in 1998, the world was taken by surprise. Not even the Israelis were aware that a ballistic missile with a range of 800 miles was already operational in Iran. And Turkey reacted very strongly to the test, revealing that it saw this event as a potential threat.

Other factors had to be taken into account. There is already a long-standing co-operation between Pyongyang and Tehran in the ballistic missile area: it was North Korea that helped Tehran during the war against Iraq, while Egypt assisted Baghdad. This co-operation may even have a nuclear dimension. Pyongyang makes no secret of its intention to sell nuclear materials or the weapons it claims to have to the highest bidder, including terrorist networks. North Korea reportedly sold uranium hexafluoride to Libya in the 1990s, via Pakistan. Tehran and Pyongyang are far apart geographically, but Pakistan and China are also countries that have well-established relations with both Iran and North Korea in the field of sensitive technologies. Finally, Iran's links with terrorism are also well documented: Tehran provides funding, training and weapons to terrorist groups in the Middle East and beyond. And the possibility of its supporting future non-conventional terrorist actions abroad is not inconceivable.

This could have sufficed to convince the Europeans to carry out their oft-repeated threat to report Iran to the Security Council in the event of a resumption of suspended activities. They did not do so in September 2005, when Iran flagrantly violated the agreement of November 2004 even though they had a majority on the IAEA Board of Governors. Nor did they do so in November 2005. This has done little for the reputation of European diplomacy, and Europe will have to shoulder part of the blame for the development of Iran's nuclear programme if the Iranian bomb sees the light of day. It shielded Iran from the Security Council on three occasions, in November 2003, November 2004, and September 2005. The outcome of this policy is becoming apparent in 2006, as Iran claims substantial technical accomplishments.

Since even the diversionary operation launched by Hizbullah on 12 July, most probably with the agreement of Iran, has not hardened the Security Council's resolve, history's judgement of the European initiatives of 2003 and 2004 may be severe. Even though the economy may be Iran's main weakness with an inflation rate close to 30% between January and August 2006, Resolution 1696 does not provide for any automatic sanctions in the event that Iran does not comply with its demands. And so everything will depend, once again, on a further decision at the end of August 2006, i.e. six months after the referral of the case to the Security Council.

3

AMERICA: IN A STATE OF PARALYSIS?

By May 2006, US policy on Iran was not yet clearly formulated. Different options still seemed to be under consideration without a specific choice having been made. Only at the very end of the month did Washington declare its readiness to negotiate with Tehran should Iran comply with the Security Council's demands. The Iranian response was not encouraging. At the end of August 2006, the most promising path to avoid the stark choice between either accepting an Iranian nuclear bomb or contemplating the use of force may be economic sanctions. Without an agreement on this point, events could prompt Washington to make a decision after the November elections, with an Iranian president close to the Revolutionary Guards, his declarations that Israel is a "tumour" in the region, the resumption of conversion and enrichment activities and its open support for Hizbullah in Lebanon. America's choice is complex as US troops are deployed in Iraq and Afghanistan where they are enduring a tough ordeal, while North Korea could take advantage of an open crisis between the USA and Iran to proceed with a nuclear test that would overturn the strategic order in the Far East. These are serious challenges, even for a country with the world's biggest army and a defence budget of over 400 billion dollars. Particularly if Washington takes into account the fact that none of the three major European powers is ready to embark on a new trial of strength in the Middle East. However, if the threat is perceived as very real, intervention, never discounted as a possibility, might well ensue to put an end to Iran's nuclear ambitions. Certainly, the argument against attacking Iran remains very persuasive. But since the possession of nuclear weapons would enable Iran to act in a still more reckless manner than now, the problem is very thorny and difficult to resolve.

1. *The shadow of the past*. For Washington, the fall of the Shah in 1979 was a political and strategic catastrophe. It was also a surprise: when President Carter took up office in 1977, he had several foreign policy priorities, but Iran was not one of them. Tehran was not expected to pose any particular problems. And so, when the Islamic revolution erupted two years later and the US Embassy was stormed on 4 November, sparking off the sadly famous hostage crisis, America had to confront one of its worst ever international situations in peacetime. During the six months that followed, the Iranian question dominated the daily meetings of the senior members of the US government, and Iran played a role of such importance throughout the latter years of Carter's presidency that it contributed to his defeat by Ronald Reagan in 1981. The Iran-Iraq war complicated relations between Tehran and Washington even further. The USA sided with Baghdad, as did all the Western countries, petrified by the Islamic peril, and did not condemn Saddam Hussein even when he used chemical weapons against the Iranian troops. Iran has also been identified as the country where the 1996 attack on the Khobar Towers American military facility in Saudi Arabia was planned. And lastly, Iran does not recognise the existence of Israel, supports Hizbullah in Lebanon, is close to Syria, is suspected of trying to stir up trouble in Iraq and Afghanistan and even of protecting members of the Al Qaeda network. From 1995, the USA has regularly renewed a regime of strict sanctions against Tehran. Diplomatic relations have never been re-established since 1979, and Washington's few diplomatic initiatives to resume relations, even at an informal level, have always failed. Iranian rhetoric on the "Great Satan" is being stoked afresh by the government, even

though it is not shared by the majority of Iran's population which is keen to open up to the west, if only for economic reasons. But the Iranian people are more excluded than ever from involvement in decisions concerning the country's affairs.

2. *The Iraq problem*. Washington's perception of the Iranian question is largely overdetermined by its perception of the Iraqi question. The Iranian agents present in Iraq have a real capacity to cause damage. The former Iraqi Prime Minister, Ibrahim Al-Jaafari, used to have links with Tehran of which he made no secret.[1] Even so, it would be mistaken to conclude that Washington will necessarily be weak in dealing with Tehran because of Iraq: the Iranian nuclear threat is too important for the USA to ignore it. When President Khatami declared in 2004 that the USA was not in a position to take "an insane decision to attack Iran" because it was "profoundly committed in Iraq", his statement had a ring of truth, but it can be misleading. If the American administration were to come to the conclusion that there is no other way of stopping the Iranian nuclear programme, especially with such an unpredictable president in Tehran, it will have no hesitation in demanding the application of sanctions, and might attack the facilities—a much more difficult choice, particularly after the 2006 war in Lebanon. An Iranian nuclear bomb could well cost a lot more than a military operation by calling into question not only America's entire "Greater Middle Eastern" policy, but also its deterrent capability in the region.

3. *The war on terrorism*. One issue over which American and Iranian interests have diverged for years is that of terrorism. Before September 11, 2001, Washington blamed Iran for the Khobar Towers attack in Saudi Arabia on 25 June 1996, which killed nineteen people. Furthermore, Iran's ongoing support for Hizbullah and Hamas is one of the region's trickiest problems, which saw a dangerous rekindling in 2006 following Tehran's tactical alliance with Damascus, the success of Hamas in the Palestinian elections, and the 12 July Hizbullah attack on Israeli territory. On the Afghan front, the situation has become

more complicated since September 11. On the one hand, the Taliban
being Iran's strategic and ideological foe, Tehran is glad to be rid of
them. On the other, the Iranian capital is regularly accused by Washington of harbouring members of Al Qaeda and is currently suspected
of planning new operations in Afghanistan.

4. *American deterrent*. So far, the Iranian regime has shown no desire to
venture onto terrain that is too risky. The new president will perhaps
set out to contradict this impression. But there is no doubt that Iran,
despite its recent arms acquisitions, including cruise and anti-aircraft
missiles, would be no match for America's weapons power. While
Washington may have good reason to think twice before attacking Tehran, the last thing the mullahs or Mahmoud Ahmadinejad can want
is a military confrontation with the United States. Consequently, if
we ask which of the two sides is most afraid of a conflict, the answer
is clear; particularly as a conflict could lead to political upheaval in
Tehran, even if the Iranian nation were to unite against an attack from
outside. As for the possibility of an Iranian attack on Israel, if that
ever were on the cards for Tehran as the new president has implied,
Washington would respond forcefully.

What is at stake for the Iranian regime is both national security and
its own survival. In principle, authoritarian regimes are conservative
by nature. They are instinctively aware of the famous Clausewitzian
concept of *friction* according to which once war has begun, nobody
can predict its development. And on the American side, after having
declared on so many occasions that an Iranian nuclear bomb would
be unacceptable, the credibility of the US's deterrence would be
undermined if Iran continued its programme with impunity. In the
run-up to the mid-term elections in the autumn of 2006, this credibility perhaps counts for less than the return of soldiers from Iraq
and Afghanistan. But that may prove an over-hasty judgement which
could be contradicted by events, if all the other solutions to halt Iran
in its race to acquire the bomb prove futile.

5. *What American policy on Iran?* In December 2004, the *Washington Post* published an editorial entitled: "We need a real Iran policy". This policy should be defined without delay if the Bush administration does not want to end up like the Carter administration, with a nuclear problem into the bargain. In Europe it is often thought that the Americans are simply waiting for the Europeans to fail before going into action. That is a possibility, but the failure is already there. The administration could invoke its long patience and the lack of success of all diplomatic efforts, including after the offer of the Six in June 2006.

Mahmoud Ahmadinejad's arrival in power, his inflammatory speeches, his determination to plough on at all costs and the feebleness of the international response to these developments all reinforce the scepticism and even the fear of some future catastrophe. Under these circumstances, America could shake off its paralysis, after a last-ditch attempt in summer 2006 to obtain a Security Council decision. America has already tried making overtures to Iran. As a matter of fact, on 31 May 2006, the Department of State proposed putting an end to what has been a constant policy towards Iran since 1979. Direct contacts between Washington and Tehran would now be possible if Iran were to accept the demands of the Board of Governors and the Security Council, i.e. the suspension of all activities associated with uranium enrichment and reprocessing. Unfortunately, Iran has not taken up this offer to date. What will follow a formal refusal in August 2006 is still undecided, but UN-imposed economic sanctions alone could badly damage the Iranian regime. Until now, Tehran has paid no price at all for its provocative policy.

4

RUSSIA: AN UNRELIABLE PARTNER

Russia is a key player in the Iran affair. Its strategic relations with Tehran are complex: the Soviet Union sided with Baghdad as did the West during the war against Iraq and at present Moscow can consider Iran as a potential threat from the south.[1] Tehran, on the other hand, has been an ally of Russia in the Caucasus region until now.[2] Furthermore, arms trade relations have built up over the last fifteen years, after a visit to Moscow in June 1989 by the then parliamentary speaker Ali Akbar Hashemi Rafsanjani. Iran notably bought Russian MiG and Sukhoi combat aircraft, T72 tanks, Kilo class diesel submarines, and surface-to-air missile systems. Russian companies also appear to be primary suppliers of Iran's ballistic missile programmes (training, testing equipment, and components).

At a press conference in Moscow in 1998, Viktor Mikhailov, one of the prime movers behind the Bushehr contract, explained the Russian government's position as follows: "What could Russia bring to the global marketplace? We had only one strength: our scientific and technological potential. Our sole chance of doing business with Iran was to help it develop nuclear power for civil purposes, where we led the field." This partnership was not confined to constructing the Bushehr reactor and supplying it with fuel, which were the subjects of contracts in 1995 and in 2005.[3] Iranian experts were trained on Russian soil, especially at the Kurchatov Institute. Russian exports

39

included essential equipment such as laser enrichment technology.[4] In January 1995, Viktor Mikhailov in person signed a draft agreement for the construction of an ultracentrifuge facility, apparently without consulting his government, and a project to provide a research reactor was cancelled in 1998 under pressure from the United States. It is possible that blueprints and operating instructions for high-performance centrifuges had also been supplied. A number of Russian institutions and some research centres entered into all kinds of partnership arrangements in the field of nuclear and ballistic weapons, without being subjected to excessive scrutiny by the central authorities. The full extent of their involvement in Iran's nuclear weapons programme is still being investigated. Moscow may be guilty of other dealings that have not come to light and might even make Russia vulnerable to blackmail by Iran, especially if corruption is involved. It is worth recalling that Yevgeny Adamov, former Minister for atomic energy, was detained in Switzerland between May 2005 and January 2006. He was accused of embezzling huge sums of American money destined to help create nuclear security in Russia, and was also suspected of having creamed off a commission on the sale of the Bushehr reactor to Iran. Both Russia and America sought his extradition, but Russia eventually succeeded in December 2005, alleging that the accused held "state secrets". It would be interesting to learn what these are. Throughout the 1990s, the United States continually pressed Moscow to adopt a more responsible nuclear policy towards Tehran. Boris Yeltsin was forced to admit the existence of a secret appendix to the Bushehr reactor agreement.[5] An American official who was well acquainted with the case under the Clinton administration wrote in autumn 2004 that "stopping Russian assistance to Iran's nuclear program was a high priority for the United States throughout much of the 1990s".[6] There was also recklessness concerning missiles, since cruise missiles with a nuclear capability sold to Iran and China by Ukraine in 1999 and 2000 were officially destined for Russia. These were Kh55 and Kh55M (also known as AF15) air-to-surface missiles launched by bombers. Iran acquired at least six of these, which would not have received export authorisations without a certificate from the Russian importer.[7] At best, it could have been an operation carried out by a Russian criminal network based in Ukraine, and at worst, a fraudulent export organised with the collusion of the Russian authorities. These missiles can play a highly destabilising role in the Persian Gulf, threatening the US 6th fleet or the ships of neighbouring states.[8] It is conceivable that this contract, diverted from its original purpose, never came to the attention of the Russian political authorities. But doubt remains because Russia had no qualms about selling arms to Tehran in the middle of the 2005-2006 crisis, and there are still signs of Russian ambiguity in many areas, despite the fact that Moscow sincerely fears Iran's acquisition of a nuclear bomb. In Moscow it is sometimes difficult to distinguish between strategic issues, commercial issues and criminal activities.

Russia supported Europe's initiatives to protect its strategic and commercial interests because it thought this was a way of delaying Iran's nuclear programme while holding on to the market for reactors and fuel. This complied with non-proliferation objectives as the fuel was to return to Russia at the end of its life cycle. But Moscow's support waned as soon as the negotiations ran into serious difficulties, despite President Putin's personal pledges to the Europeans and the Israelis.[9] In December 2005, when Tehran rejected Moscow's offer to proceed with uranium enrichment in Russia, some observers believed this was the last straw and that Russia would take a harder line. This was not the case. Igor Ivanov merely asked Tehran to take a slightly more conciliatory attitude, and the upshot a few days later was a promise by Iran's chief negotiator, Ali Larijani, to examine the Russian proposal.[10] This committed him to nothing, but it enabled Iran to gain precious time. Before (and during) the Board of Governors in March 2006, there were persistent rumours of a last-minute deal between Russia and Iran that would result in Tehran being allowed to keep a small-scale enrichment pilot facility on Iranian soil. These rumours were denied by Moscow. But after the Board meeting, Iran having rejected the Russian proposal time and time again, there was no relaxation of Moscow's position in New York, not even over the adoption of a straightforward presidential declaration by the Security Council: it still took three weeks to adopt the presidential statement in March. And in July, Moscow made sure there would be no automatic sanctions if Tehran refused to comply with UNSC resolution 1696.

1. *A more reliable partner than in the past?* This is what the Europeans initially thought, before taking a harsher view in summer 2005. Russia had clearly played a part in helping Iran pursue its nuclear ambitions up until the 1990s. A change was noted in autumn 2002, probably because Moscow could no longer ignore the new factors that were then emerging. The question was whether the Russian authorities had issued specific instructions, particularly to Minatom, the atomic energy Ministry, to be more vigilant than in the past. The February 2005 fuel contract was not signed by Moscow until Iran had provided some non-proliferation guarantees.[11] The Europeans saw it as support for, and even a concrete contribution to, their diplomatic efforts. If the Bushehr reactor is to start operating by the end of 2006, the fuel would need to be delivered six months beforehand, but it had still not arrived by August, because of the current crisis. The IAEA is supposed to monitor the use of this fuel and the installations where it will be in circulation, but if Iran decides to terminate the international inspections after delivery by the Russians, what use could Iran make of it? Diverting it for military applications would lead to stormy relations between Tehran and Moscow, but the technical assurance that this fuel will not be diverted has not exactly been forthcoming. It is therefore justifiable to ask Moscow to continue to suspend delivery of fuel supplies, especially after the IAEA resolution of 4 February 2006, the Security Council presidential declaration of March 2006, and the adoption of resolution 1696 by the UNSC. Most member states of the Nuclear Suppliers Group (NSG) are agreed that there can be no

nuclear co-operation with a country that is in violation of its non-proliferation obligations, and this message is addressed to Russia.[12]

2. *Moscow has no doubts as to Iran's weapons ambitions.* The conclusion reached by Russia's highest authorities concerning Iran's intentions is no longer a mystery to the rest of the world: Moscow is convinced that Tehran wants to develop nuclear weapons. Russia has accurately interpreted Iran's attempts to purchase isostatic presses and vacuum furnaces. It is also aware of the significance of casting and machining of uranium metal into hemispherical forms. Furthermore, Russia's internal sources can add to the many indications given in IAEA reports. Moscow is much better informed than the West about some of Iran's sensitive imports, and maybe even about some undisclosed sites.[13] After all, so many experts from Minatom/Rosatom and other Russian bodies have visited Iran in the last fifteen years that it cannot be otherwise. The Russians, no amateurs when it comes to intelligence, probably have an interesting dossier on Iran's nuclear programme. A full exchange of intelligence, with Moscow sharing the information in its possession, would constitute a mark of trust towards the Europeans and the Americans. But it is hard to envisage, given the revelations on past Russian-Iranian relations that would emerge. It is probably this fear that at least partially explains Moscow's often ambiguous declarations on the nature of Iran's nuclear programme. In January 2005 for example, when foreign minister Sergei Lavrov stated: "I have no reason to believe that the situation is developing in an abnormal way or that the peaceful character of Iran's nuclear programme is going to change," it was not clear what he meant. A month later, in February, President Putin in person however echoed his words, declaring just before the signature of the fuel contract that there were no signs of a nuclear weapons programme in Iran.

3. *Moscow recognises the Iranian threat, but is maintaining an ambiguous public stance on the issue.* Despite Sergei Lavrov and Vladimir Putin's optimism, a number of indications show that Moscow has no serious doubt about Tehran's ambitions. The question is whether Russia

adapted its policy to this awareness, and whether Washington's support for democratic movements in the neighbouring republics did not create new tensions over the Iranian dossier in the last two years. The Russian elections are set for 2008, a date that will determine many decisions, some of them having a strategic nature. Iran fears a "betrayal", and continues to play for time.

As long as Moscow refuses to acknowledge the military nature of the programme, or to discuss "red lines" that Iran cannot be permitted to cross under any circumstances,[14] no one can foresee what Russia's attitude will be at the Security Council at the end of August 2006. And yet Moscow's backing there is vital, especially given China's weak support.[15] For the time being, Moscow's clearest public statement is the one made at the Evian G8 summit in June 2003, when Iran was called upon in strong terms to sign and ratify the Additional Protocol to its Safeguards Agreement with the IAEA, allowing more comprehensive access to the sites, personnel and documents. In 2006, the declarations of the Saint Petersburg summit on Iran could have carried a greater weight, especially after the resolution that was adopted in Paris on 12 July — by the foreign ministers of China, France, Germany, Russia, the United Kingdom, and the United States, along with the high representative of the European Union — but they were overshadowed by the Lebanon crisis.

4. *Russia should clarify its position.* It is futile to criticise the contract signed in 2005 between Moscow and Tehran allowing Russia to supply fuel, as it underlines the pointlessness of Iran's having an autonomous fuel cycle. The necessary replacement of the heavy-water research reactor at Arak with a light-water reactor considered less likely to be misused for weapons purposes can also give priority to the provision of a Russian-made facility. Moscow's important role must be acknowledged, and if strategic fuel stocks are envisaged in a third-party country, Russia should be consulted on the best methods. In exchange, Moscow must not allow there to be any ambiguity as to the nature of the "Russian proposal" to enrich fuel on Russian soil or as to

its stance at the Security Council if Iran does not comply. There could be no question, for example, of maintaining conversion activities in Iran. There are at least two reasons for this, one technical, since the hexafluoride produced might not be adequate for enrichment in Russia, and the other strategic, as allowing the Isfahan facility to remain operational would make it impossible to provide the requisite non-proliferation safeguards.[16] Hence, at the annual Munich Conference on Security Policy in Europe, the Russian Minister of defence, Sergei Ivanov, declared on 5 February 2006 that the "Russian proposal" would include neither conversion nor enrichment on Iranian soil. But these words have never been reiterated by Moscow.

A few months earlier, in May 2005, at the Review Conference of the Parties to the Treaty on the Non-Proliferation of Nuclear Weapons held in New York, the Russian delegation played a key role in obstructing a text by the five nuclear powers (who are also the five permanent members of the Security Council) which would have mentioned Iran. Moscow's instructions were to avoid any reference to Tehran during this exercise. Russia was doubtless under tremendous pressure from Iran: any text from the "Five" could be seen as a prelude to a Security Council resolution. It is also noteworthy that at the same time, President Putin was the first head of state to congratulate the new Iranian president. When the Board of Governors' resolution was carried on 11 August 2005, Russia created last-minute complications: according to Moscow the date of 3 September set for the IAEA report, already very late, was likely to result in another Board of Governors' extraordinary meeting on Iran just prior to the New York summit on the future of the United Nations. Russia had to be assured that the adoption of the text did not prejudice the holding of a Board meeting, which in fact did not take place. But this concession did not lead to Moscow being more cooperative at the meeting of 19 September. Despite the assurances given during the summer, Moscow was opposed to bringing in the Security Council and would not recognise that Iran had "violated" its obligations. The Russian delegation abstained from

the vote of September 2005. In autumn 2005, despite the emergence
of new information concerning Iran's possession of documents on
uranium metal casting and machining, Moscow continued to advocate dialogue. In February 2006, Russia agreed to vote on the resolution only after obtaining assurances that the Security Council would
merely be "informed" at this stage. And Russia's attitude in New York
in March and July is open to various interpretations.

5. *Moscow considers Iran an important partner in the Middle East.* The
present poor relations between Russia and the United States are a
boon for Russia, helping it forge a special bond with Tehran. This may
contradict other aspects of Russian policy, but it is not Moscow's only
inconsistency. In view of the serious rivalry with China in central Asia,
despite the surface agreements that exist within the Shanghai group,[17]
Moscow's return to the Middle East via Iran is an understandable
temptation, especially as there are important commercial interests at
stake: after Bushehr 1, Moscow would effectively build Bushehr 2
and Bushehr 3 if a comprehensive agreement could be concluded with
Iran.[18] For this reason, the Iranians tie any strategic partnership with
Russia to the pursuit of nuclear co-operation. This continues to hold
true, and it is hard to have a clear idea of what would make Moscow
give due consideration to its obligations as a depositary of the NPT.
Over time, Russia has once more become an ambiguous partner with
regard to Iran. It is not impossible that Moscow will do all it can
in August to avoid a formal discussion on actual sanctions. But Te-
hran has become so intransigent that it can also force Moscow to be
tougher. We should get to the bottom of this in the coming months.
In summer 2006, Russian policy was still ambiguous, even after the
Lebanon crisis which showed Tehran's increased nuisance capability.
Agreement on Resolution 1696 of 31 July was only obtained in New
York on the express condition that Iran's non-compliance with the
Security Council's demand would not necessarily result in sanctions.

5

CHINA: A CLOSE ALLY FOR IRAN

Over the last few decades[1] China has forged close links with Iran and its co-operation with Tehran has increased considerably since the 1980s thanks to China's insatiable energy needs and to Iran's appetite for weapons and consumer goods.[2] There is also a military aspect to this partnership, with the Islamic Republic gaining increasing access to the technologies and weapons developed and used by the People's Liberation Army. There are further reasons for an Iranian-Chinese alliance: the hostility of both countries towards the United States, the need for Iran to preserve an "oriental alternative" to rapprochement with the west, and the role model that China represents for Tehran. Lastly, in the long term, Iran might play a still unforeseen role if a conflict flares up between China and the United States over Taiwan, especially if by that time Tehran has a nuclear deterrent. Both countries have an interest in controlling shipping routes between the Middle East and Asia. And for the time being, it is in the Chinese interest to maintain a tricky problem for the United States very much to the west of China.[3]

Nuclear co-operation with China is one of the most significant alliances Iran has established, alongside those with Russia and Pakistan. Large numbers of Chinese nuclear experts have spent time in Iran, and the international inspectors have noted that their arrival in Iran was often preceded by the hurried departure of Chinese scientists and technicians, who vanished from the sites being inspected for the duration of their visit. So far, Beijing's support for Tehran has been unwavering, but this does not mean that China is prepared to encourage any form of Iranian venture. Beijing's interest is rather for the negotiations to drag on indefinitely, without any decision being reached as to whether to act at the Security Council. China has similar ambitions regarding North Korea: prolong the discussions and defer the crisis for as long as possible. Meanwhile, the dream of Iran's conservatives may well be to follow the Chinese model of combining economic liberalisation and political repression.

1. *Numerous arms deals.* Iran has imported key defence components from China, in particular some 60 anti-ship missiles (with a 75-mile range and a speed of 0.9 Mach), capable of posing a serious threat to both commercial and military vessels in the region. These missiles are more sophisticated than the better known Chinese H2-Y "Silkworm" cruise missile (55-mile range), which Iran has deployed extensively along its coasts and on the island of Abu Musa in the middle of the Persian Gulf. These two types of missiles, in addition to the Kilo submarines[4] purchased from Russia, give Iran a high damage capability, threatening both warships and commercial vessels, and enhance its strategic superiority over its neighbours. Iran also acquired powerful surveillance radar equipment from China in the mid-1990s, permitting ultramodern tactical surveillance as part of an automated air defence system. In both cases, it seems that elements of American technology, bought by China, might also be integrated into this equipment. And lastly, China has helped Iran in the field of ballistics by selling it a large number of guidance systems, a technology which Iran has not developed. China may see arms sales to Iran as retribution for US arms sales to Taiwan. It also wants to guarantee oil supplies and earn revenue from weapons sales.

Furthermore, Beijing is suspected of using North Korea as an intermediary for transfers of ballistic missile technology rather than delivering it directly. A transfer of this kind via Russia was reported in the press in October 2005.[5]

2. *Clandestine nuclear co-operation.* Nuclear co-operation agreements between Iran and China were signed in January 1990 and September 1992. One of the initial revelations in the IAEA reports (in February 2003) was China's exportation of nuclear materials in 1991 which neither Iran nor China declared to the IAEA before 2003, i.e. twelve years after the conclusion of the deal. These exports comprised of natural uranium in three different forms, UF_6 (1000 kg), UF_4 (400 kg) and UO_2 (400 kg), stored at the Tehran nuclear research centre. Iran was forced to acknowledge that the UF_4 had been entirely converted into uranium metal, which is useful for producing weapons but much less for civil purposes. On several occasions, intelligence concerning the presence of Chinese and North Korean experts and the help they provided for Iran's nuclear programme emerged in different countries. Some 50 Chinese experts were apparently observed at the Saghand uranium mine, particularly at the time a laser enrichment facility was being installed. China also sought to export Qinshan-type nuclear power plants to Iran. But as these required numerous foreign components, mainly French, German and Japanese, they could not be re-exported from China without the consent of the countries of origin. That was how Russia finally won the Bushehr contract and secured the market for nuclear power stations in Iran. The main obstacle to the Chinese contract seems in fact to have come from Iran itself: the envisaged site was close to the Iraqi border and Tehran feared a repetition of the Bushehr bombing of 1983. After Iran asked China to select a second site near the Persian Gulf, the project collapsed for reasons that have never really been clarified. However, in 1995, China sold Iran a Tokamak fusion research reactor using beryllium and tritium which was installed in Tehran and could in principle enable Iran to carry out some testing useful for thermonuclear devices. This facility is rarely mentioned in IAEA reports, despite its role in tests which could be directly linked to the weapons programme.

3. *Sales of chemical and biological precursors*. The sale by China of precursors for Iran's chemical and biological weapons programmes came to the attention of observers around a decade ago. In 1996, the *Washington Post* reported that Chinese companies were supplying complete chemical weapons plants to Iran. These imports were destined for the army, which left little doubt as to the ultimate use of the products and equipment in question. Comparable intelligence was available relating to biological weapons. Because Iran was a signatory to the Chemical Weapons Convention, Tehran had to provide The Hague with a comprehensive declaration of its stockpiles and sites. This declaration is still incomplete today. But no comparable verification mechanism exists at this stage in the biological weapons area.

4. *Political ties*. China seems in many ways to be a role model for Iran's conservatives. It has achieved economic modernisation while maintaining political control over its population. After Iran's supreme leader Ayatollah Khamenei destroyed the pro-reform opposition with —it is sometimes forgotten—the help of ex-president Rafsanjani,[6] the Chinese model was held up as an example. Could it be transposed to Iran? That was another matter. Be that as it may, links between Iran and China were also strengthened by America's hostility towards both countries. In February 2001, at the beginning of the Bush administration, China and Iran were both on an American list of foes of the United States, and the situation has barely improved since.

5. *China's energy needs and the potential role of Iran in the event of a conflict over Taiwan*. One reason why Iran is of major strategic importance for China is its oil and gas reserves. China now imports 40% of its oil and in 2004 it became the world's second largest consumer country. The same year, 15% of its oil imports came from Iran, and China signed a 70-billion-dollar contract to purchase Iranian oil and gas. Moreover, it is no secret that China is cultivating close relations in the Middle East (Iran, Saudi Arabia), in Africa (Sudan and Zimbabwe) and in South America (Venezuela) for energy reasons. But oil and gas are not the only motive for the close ties between Beijing and Tehran,

especially from a long-term perspective. China may arm Iran in order to divert some US forces from areas near Taiwan. And in the event of a conflict between China and Taiwan, Iran could play an important role supporting Beijing in the Middle East, as could Pakistan, which has an even closer relationship with China. Relations between Iran and Pakistan are very hard to fathom. At times they seem to be very fraught,[7] at others it appears as though Islamabad is protecting Tehran from international prying, probably to avoid giving too much away about its own past nuclear co-operation.[8] This is discussed in the next chapter.

6. *Has China ended all nuclear co-operation with Iran?* Direct co-operation, probably yes, but indirect co-operation cannot be ruled out. A number of observers consider that if Iran already has a blueprint for a bomb, even if acquired through a Pakistani intermediary, it probably originated in China, like the one Pakistan offered Iraq in 1990 and Libya a few years later. In this case, Beijing would be in blatant violation of its NPT obligations. The nuclear powers effectively undertake not to assist states that do not have nuclear weapons to acquire them, either directly or indirectly. But this would only apply if the transfer took place after August 1992, when China signed up to the NPT, and that is unlikely. Very recently, Chinese land transports between the Baluch region of west Pakistan and Iran came to the attention of observers of the region, and Beijing's discretion concerning Iran's case could very well be closely linked to an effective pursuit of a strategic partnership. At the Security Council in any case, Beijing remains a fairly close ally of Tehran, by continually deferring the deadlines and restricting the scope of the draft resolutions submitted to it. And in August 2006, China still declared that it opposed sanctions against Iran because "they cannot solve the problems", leaving observers wondering what could "fully" solve them according to the Chinese.

6

PAKISTAN: CLANDESTINE SUPPLIER, UNEASY NEIGHBOUR

Ambiguity surrounds relations between Iran and Pakistan. There have been periods of tactical alliance, for example when the Shah helped President Ali Bhutto to crush the Baluch rebels in the 1970s. But since the Islamic revolution of 1979 and the Taliban's arrival in power in Afghanistan, Iran and Pakistan have moved apart. The Taliban were the declared enemy of Tehran, at both strategic and ideological levels.[1] More recently, in the late 1990s, there were periods of outright hostility between Iran and Pakistan.[2] But at different periods, exchanges of sensitive equipment, including nuclear-related technology, took place between the two countries, particularly in the 1980s and 1990s. It is difficult, even now, to gauge the full extent of that co-operation. But there is no doubt that in the late 1980s, General Aslam Beg, the chief of staff of the Pakistani army, decided to enter into a strategic co-operation with Iran. One of the most incriminating elements of the IAEA dossier on Iran is a nuclear offer from Pakistan dated 1987 and which Tehran acknowledges.[3] A decade later, in the mid-1990s, Abdul Qadeer Khan's clandestine network supplied Iran with blueprints for first-generation P1 centrifuges and second-generation P2 centrifuges. Since the revelation of the links between Iran and Pakistan, their relations have sometimes been strained. Islamabad was forced to reveal that it had provided clandestine supplies to Tehran as it had done to Libya, an admission it would rather not have had to make and which prompted the international inspectors to request access to closed sites.[4] Tehran for its part felt betrayed by Islamabad, particularly when the Pakistani authorities were obliged to explain their activities in Iran to the American intelligence services and the IAEA and to hand over to the Vienna Agency centrifuge components similar to those sold to Iran, which they did after prolonged delays. But there are important limits to Pakistan's co-operation with the IAEA, since the inspectors have still not been granted the necessary access to its nuclear sites that would enable them to confirm their conclusions. Consequently, there is no way of verifying Iran and Pakistan's statements on the crucial question of centrifuge components contaminated with enriched uranium. The components provided by Islamabad may or may not have come from Pakistani sites.

1. *The discovery of the relationship between Iran and Pakistan.* From the moment Iran admitted that its programme was based on Urenco technology,[5] denying all the while that it had co-operated with Islamabad, the IAEA launched an investigation into possible links between the two countries. Effectively, the Pakistani programme has the same origin, Dr Abdul Qadeer Khan having stolen Urenco blueprints for two uranium centrifuges from the Almelo enrichment facility in the Netherlands. It was Libya's revelations that loosened tongues, both in Tehran and Islamabad. On 2 February 2004, Pakistan, under pressure to make a statement and anxious to protect its own interests, published a written confession by AQ Khan admitting to having passed on information and ultracentrifuge equipment to Tehran, Tripoli and Pyongyang.

Iran is also alleged to have received technologies and components between 1989 and 1991, and a production unit in Malaysia is thought to have been involved in recycling Pakistani equipment. A few days later, the IAEA discovered that Iran had acquired blueprints for centrifuges more sophisticated than those at Natanz (P1 centrifuges) via the Pakistani network. This information had been divulged during the dismantling of the clandestine Libyan nuclear programme, and the trail led back to Iran. Iran admits to being in possession of these plans, which have so far remained undisclosed. Abu Tahir, a financial go-between from the Khan Research Laboratories network, confesses to having organised the delivery of two containers of centrifuge components from Pakistan to Iran, via Dubai, in 1994-1995, at the request of Abdul Qadeer Khan. These centrifuges, Iran confirmed in January 2004, underwent mechanical trials (without nuclear materials, according to Tehran).[6] Iran also confirms having purchased nuclear equipment from Pakistani intermediaries during the same period. These declarations, which followed those of Colonel Gaddafi, led the observers to conclude that the AQ Khan network had indeed had dealings with Iran.

2. *The 1987 offer.* During the international investigation into Pakistan's nuclear programme, a certain number of clues convinced the IAEA inspectors of the existence of an offer from Pakistan to Iran in the late 1980s. Tehran was presented with a firm demand to hand over the original document or at least a complete copy. Iran has always maintained that this document did not exist and produced only a brief description focusing mainly on an offer of centrifuge technology. This episode is described as follows by Pierre Goldschmidt, the IAEA's former Head of Safeguards, in his report of 1st March 2005:

During a meeting on 12 January 2005 in Tehran, Iran showed the Agency a hand-written one-page document reflecting an offer said to have been made to Iran in 1987 by a foreign intermediary. While it is not entirely clear from the document precisely what the offer entailed, Iran has stated that it related to centrifuge technology acquisition. This document suggests that the offer included the delivery of: a disassembled sample machine (including drawings, descriptions, and specifications for production); drawings, specifications and calculations for a "complete plant"; and materials for 2000 centrifuge machines. The document also reflects an offer to provide auxiliary vacuum and electric drive equipment and uranium re-conversion and casting capabilities. Iran stated that only some of these items had been delivered, and that all of those items had been declared to the IAEA. This information is still being assessed. The Agency has requested that all documentation relevant to the offer be made available for the Agency's review.[7]

In his report to the Board of Governors of 16 June 2005, Pierre Goldschmidt added that this handwritten page had "no date, names, signatures or addresses". This information has not been forthcoming since, and Pakistan, which logically should have a copy of the offer, has not provided more detailed information on this subject.

3. *Pakistan's co-operation with the IAEA.* Apart from the incomplete nature of the document handed over to the IAEA by Iran in connection with the 1987 offer, one of the main unanswered questions concerns the source of the traces of enriched uranium found on Iranian soil since February 2003. If, as Iran claims, it is simply contaminated equipment sold by Pakistan, Tehran could be exonerated (on condition that all the levels of enrichment found by the inspectors can be thus explained).[8] If, on the other hand, tests show that the types of enrichment (or some of them) do not corroborate this assertion, it will be proven not only that Iran lied, but furthermore that enrichment activities have taken place on Iranian soil over and above those declared to the IAEA. If very high levels of unexplained enrichment were to transpire, it would go without saying that activities that have no civil purpose have taken place in Iran. This would be a blatant violation of the Safeguards Agreement. Until 2005, Pakistan refused to hand over the components that would make it possible to carry out the comparative analyses, even if the IAEA had "agreed with the Member State concerned"[9] on the modalities for sampling a number of old centrifuge components, which could provide information on the origin of the low-enriched and high-enriched uranium particle contamination found at various locations in Iran".[10] It was only in January and then in May 2005, after two years of procrastination, that the items requested from Pakistan reached the IAEA. The intervening time could have been used by Islamabad to ensure that nothing was handed over to

Vienna that might bring the Pakistani authorities into disrepute. The IAEA's confirmation that it had received the centrifuge components and samples of enriched uranium[11] coincided with a meeting between the three European foreign ministers and their Iranian counterpart in Geneva.[12] On this occasion, Tehran agreed to defer carrying out its threat to resume uranium conversion activities, brandished throughout the month of May in the run-up to the elections. This "flexibility" can perhaps be explained by the Pakistani decision to co-operate with the IAEA. But the source of the components in Vienna's possession is impossible to determine for sure, and the Russian, American, Japanese, British and French experts gathered in the Austrian capital in late August 2005 were unable to reach any definite conclusions. The uncertainty as to the components' origins is only one of the reasons for this situation, another being the contradictions and inconsistencies in Pakistan's declarations. Furthermore, these components having, in theory, been stored for some time in Dubai before reaching Iran, it is interesting to note that no traces of enriched uranium were found in the warehouse used. Granted, the report of 27 February 2006, paragraph 8 offers an explanation for this absence (change of owner), albeit a very cautious and inconclusive one. In his report of February 2006, the new Head of Safeguards, Olli Heinonen, wrote that the IAEA is still seeking explanations for some of the traces of low-enriched and high-enriched uranium found on Iranian soil. By August 2006, still no explanation has been forthcoming.

4. *A deal between Pakistan and the United States?* Despite denials from both countries, it was thought for a while that Washington and Islamabad had possibly struck a deal according to which President Musharraf would provide the American administration with the information required on Iran in exchange for a promise not to be asked to hand over Abdul Qadeer Khan to be questioned directly about his nuclear trafficking network. But no confirmation has ever been available.

At the end of May 2005, there were also rumours of a declaration by President Musharraf supposedly asserting that Iran was "very keen to have the bomb", a clear statement that Washington would have welcomed. Tehran, outraged, demanded an immediate explanation.[13] But subsequent developments show much more clearly that Pakistan will do nothing that might damage Tehran, mainly because any revelation would call into question its own past doings, and even its links with China.

5. *Pakistan is no longer "proliferating" in Iran.* This by no means indicates that all past relations have been divulged, especially if we bear in mind that three chiefs of staff of the Pakistani army, *including General Musharraf*, are probably implicated. Pakistan remains key to understanding Iran's past and present nuclear activities, whether it is a question of equipment contaminated with low- or high-enriched uranium, the Pakistani offer of 1987 of which the IAEA is unable to obtain either the original or a complete copy, or the reported sale of enriched uranium in 2001, which the Iranian opposition spoke of at a press conference in Paris in 2004, without producing evidence. Why would Pakistan co-operate with the IAEA to resolve these questions, when the United States itself was keeping quiet so as not to undermine its ally Musharraf? Hence, Pakistan has given the IAEA little assistance, and has even proffered contradictory explanations. The inspectors being unable to take samples on site,[14] it is impossible for them to determine the origins of the components handed over to Vienna. It is conceivable that they could just as well have come from Iran. But although Islamabad has only co-operated with the IAEA in a limited way — possibly because it had a "prior agreement" with Tehran on some points — it is highly unlikely that the Pakistani capital will continue to assist Iran's proliferation activities.

7

INDIA: ENERGY NEEDS AND
RAPPROCHEMENT WITH WASHINGTON

India's relations with Iran date back hundreds of years, and Persian influence is still evident in art and architecture throughout the north of the country. Nehru wrote: "Among the many peoples and races who have come in contact with and influenced India's life and culture, the oldest and most persistent have been the Iranians".[1] Today, Iran and India are also the world's two main Shia Muslim countries.[2] New Delhi has maintained an ambiguous attitude towards Iran's nuclear case which can be explained in three different ways.

1. *Relations between India and Iran are satisfactory.* There are no disputes between them. New Delhi is keen to preserve these relations for strategic reasons, because of the help it has received—so far—from Iran in Afghanistan, and because of the possibility of entering into a reverse alliance against Pakistan (Iran has given much more help to Afghanistan for years, but this could change in 2006 if the prospect of Security Council action becomes more likely). There is also an energy motive, since India is heavily dependent on Iranian oil and gas, given the size of its population and its very rapidly growing economy.[3] It is one of the reasons why Washington—the Bush administration merely pursuing an avenue opened by the Clinton administration—has been attempting for years to persuade Congress to agree to the sale of nu-

clear reactors to India, so as to reduce its energy dependency on Iran. An interview with Robert Blackwill in *The National Interest*, in June 2005, clearly explains this approach and the reasons behind it. The decision to put this policy into practice announced a month later, with the almost immediate assent of the Director General of the IAEA will lead to the transfer of civil nuclear reactors to India becoming a *fait accompli*, now that the American Congress has ratified the deal.[4] As for Iran, forging a series of diplomatic, economic and military alliances is part of its strategy to counter US threats, in which India could have a key role. For the time being, Iran and India's military relations remain very limited (confined chiefly to joint naval exercises), but the declaration between Tehran and New Delhi signed in January 2003 was more ambitious and covered energy as well as strategic and military issues. Lastly, New Delhi cannot ignore the fact that India is home to 25 million Shia Muslims.

2. *The Iran-Pakistan-India natural gas pipeline*. A project dear to the Indians, some observers are convinced it is the reason behind New Delhi's former support for Tehran. Initially came the discovery of natural gas reserves in the Persian Gulf, in 1988 (the year the war with Iraq ended), and Iran's wish to exploit them and export gas.[5] India and Pakistan were both the most natural potential customers since their gas reserves are low and their energy needs continually increasing.[6] In 1995, Iran and Pakistan signed a preliminary agreement in Karachi for the construction of the Pars pipeline. Then, Tehran proposed extending the pipeline to India, passing through Pakistan. At first, India expressed reservations about this solution which would create a dependency on Islamabad. It would have preferred a new, underwater pipeline between Iran and India. But an agreement was finally signed in January 2005 for the delivery of 7.5 million tonnes of natural gas a year, for a period of 25 years (at a cost of 64 billion dollars). According to this contract, confirmed by a new agreement on 17 February 2005, the gas pipeline will pass through Pakistan.[7] In February 2006, Pakistan declared that nothing was definite yet.

This project did not stop India from voting for the IAEA resolution condemning Iran in September 2005. Nor did this vote have any effect on the gas contract, showing at least that Iran needs to sell its gas as much as India needs to buy it. Again, in February 2006, India voted in favour of the Director General of the IAEA resolution to refer Iran's case to the Security Council. In fact, India does not want, at any cost, to be seen as the "baddie" on the non-proliferation issue. India's July 2005 agreement with the USA on nuclear co-operation for peaceful purposes, ratified by the American Congress in July 2006 and hailed by many as an important victory for New Delhi, may also curb Iran's ambitions to influence India's foreign policy.

3. *India does not want to defend too openly a treaty (the NPT) which it does not recognise.* This is a more political factor, which is quite complex. India has always been vehemently against the NPT, which recognises China as a nuclear power but not India. Effectively, this 1968 treaty only recognises as states with nuclear arms those which had carried out a nuclear explosion prior to January 1967. This includes China (1964), but India waited until 1974 to conduct its first test, described as "peaceful" at the time, though this deceived no one. Since the underground nuclear explosions of May 1998, the situation has become completely clear: India is a *de facto* nuclear power, not recognised by the NPT, but New Delhi knows that the death of the NPT—particularly on its doorstep—would not serve its security interests. India, unlike Pakistan, has always conducted a responsible foreign nuclear policy. The two researchers accused for a time by the USA of having helped Iran with its nuclear programme (in particular with building heavy-water reactors) were eventually exonerated.[8] But it is not impossible that India's hostility to the NPT, which stems from an ideological position, is influencing India's policy on Iran insofar as India feels it has been subjected to the same western pressures as Tehran. However the shifts in Delhi's position in 2005 and 2006 would seem to suggest that India supports a policy of non-proliferation, and is even

wary of Iran's intentions and the strategic consequences of Tehran's acquisition of the nuclear bomb.

4. *India considers that Pakistan has not paid any price for its proliferation policy*. This is a powerful argument. India is at the forefront of countries taken aback at the leniency of the international community—and of the United States in particular—towards Islamabad. Already shocked that Washington was seeking a rapprochement with Islamabad in the name of the war on terrorism, of which India has been one of the main victims over the last twenty years, New Delhi finds it unacceptable that the exposure of the Abdul Qadeer Khan network did not result in any sanctions. Particularly as in India, and the rest of the world, there is little doubt that the Pakistani army and intelligence services colluded in the network's activities.[9] New Delhi therefore finds it unjustifiable, even unjust, to put such pressure on Iran, which in its view of events has so far caused much less damage to the non-proliferation regime than Pakistan.

5. *New Delhi's leniency towards Tehran does have its limits, however*. Iran tried hard to convince India, in particular before the May 2005 Review Conference of the Parties to the Treaty on the Non-Proliferation of Nuclear Weapons, that the two countries were in a similar situation: the Western countries were preventing them from having access to technology and even wanted to halt nuclear development work in both of their countries. But New Delhi immediately pointed out to Tehran, not without some condescension, that India had never signed the Non-Proliferation Treaty, and that its policy has always been to abide by its international obligations. Consequently, if Iran violated its IAEA Safeguards Agreement or even the NPT directly, it could not count on support from India. This position is all the more adamant as New Delhi does not want to have a new nuclear power within range. This explains India's attitude to Iran since September 2005 and its "yes" vote on the question of referring Iran's nuclear case to the Security Council in February 2006.

6. *The joint declaration of 18 July 2005 by India and America can re-inforce this position even further.* One of George W. Bush's greatest ambitions is to bring about a rapprochement between India and the United States.[10] His main objective is to pave the way for a century whose centre of gravity will be in Asia, and create the best possible strategic conditions for Washington. But as part of this overall policy, the decision to enter into a civil nuclear energy pact so as to diversify India's energy resources, breaks with a *de facto* policy to impose a nuclear embargo.[11] This embargo policy is linked to India's refusal to sign the NPT as well as to the nuclear tests it carried out in 1998. Some politicians and experts in India still oppose the ratification of the agreement with the US, claiming that it represents a constraint on the development of India's nuclear arsenal in the years to come, in particular vis-à-vis China. From the US point of view, as we said earlier, relaxing its hardline policy would also be a way for Washington to prevent New Delhi from being too dependent on Tehran for energy. But influential voices in Congress also fear that this agreement might jeopardise America's non-proliferation policy, and in particular Washington's tireless support for the Group of Nuclear Suppliers which opposes this agreement, despite the support of the Director General of the IAEA. This Group includes China, which is not prepared to make any concessions either to India or the United States.

7. *The Chinese reaction to this rapprochement is revealing.* Surprisingly, on the international scene, Beijing alone understood Tehran's announcement that it was resuming its activities on 1 August 2005 as a reaction to the Indian-American declaration. Even if Tehran's policy has little connection to this new development in bilateral relations between New Delhi and Washington, Beijing's interpretation speaks volumes about its hostility to America's new policy towards India. A few months later, China announced that an agreement between Washington and Delhi would result in a similar nuclear partnership between Beijing and Islamabad. Given the military nature of past

nuclear relations between China and Pakistan, the warning with regard to India was not even veiled. But wisely, the Indian authorities
did not react to these threats

8

ISRAEL: AN EXISTENTIAL THREAT

Israel, it must be stressed, is not the reason why Tehran wants to acquire the nuclear bomb. The key dates when decisions were made, i.e. the 1970s under the Shah, who had good relations with Israel, and then 1985 during the war with Iraq, suggest that there was a different agenda. In the 1970s, it was a desire for regional domination, and in the 1980s, the wish to acquire a decisive response to Saddam Hussein's lethal chemical weapons attacks on Iranian troops that had been going on since 1983. But if Israel is not the reason for Iran's nuclear programme, it provides Iran with an excellent justification to give its neighbours, since Tehran cannot be too overt about Iran's regional ambitions at the start of the twenty-first century. The Israeli nuclear arsenal being moreover a permanent source of irritation and even frustration in the Arab world, it is an easy way of countering the Arab capitals' objections.[1] That said, Tehran is fully aware that all dread the appearance of an Iranian nuclear bomb, especially in the Gulf.

Faced with this situation, Tel Aviv's official position on Iran's nuclear programme is both clear and succinct: it consists chiefly of reminding the world that the State of Israel has the capability to defend itself if one of its neighbours were to attack. It is a way of evoking the array of conventional and non-conventional means Israel has at its disposal: a highly efficient air capability, some of the most sophisticated anti-missile systems in the world (notably the Arrow system),

65

and a nuclear arsenal which, although undeclared, is however seen by the rest of the world as a serious deterrent. The stance of Israeli diplomats, experts and politicians on the issue has always been deliberately moderate, both to let Iran take responsibility for its aggressive attitude, and to remind the world that Israel's substantial military resources should cause any potential enemy to think twice.

That said, it is hard for the Israeli government to view the way the situation has evolved with equanimity, particularly after the July 2006 Hizbullah attack in the north of the country. Since the early 1990s, Israelis leaders have taken the Iranian threat seriously. Tel Aviv, like Washington, tried in vain for over a decade to alert the Western capitals to Tehran's nuclear activities. After three years of international inspections and the revelations concerning Abdul Qadeer Khan's clandestine Pakistani network, they were vindicated by the facts, which perhaps surpassed what the Israeli intelligence services knew. Besides, Iran's increasing involvement in terrorist activities against Israel is an additional worrying factor which could become more alarming if Iran counter-attacks after becoming the subject of more serious discussions at the Security Council in 2006. And finally, it is clear that the new Iranian president is a source of fresh anxiety, not only because he is a man of confrontation and not of compromise, but also because he openly claims to want to "wipe Israel from the map", calling it a "tumour". One may wonder about the effectiveness of a nuclear deterrent against an individual who uses such rhetoric. Deterrence presupposes a sound knowledge of the enemy, but also some kind of mutual recognition. If the ambition is to wipe a country from the map, then the deterrence relationship will be much harder to build.

That is how many observers and Israeli politicians have come to consider Tehran as the main menace Israel may have to confront in the coming years and decades. Iran is even seen as a threat that can jeopardise the existence of the State of Israel, as has occurred at two points in the country's history: in 1948 when it was founded and during the Yom Kippur war of 1973, when attack on Israel came as a major surprise. Before Mahmoud Ahmadinejad's declarations which outraged the entire world,[2] the annual military parades in Tehran already sent out sufficiently worrying signals: the missiles were usually adorned with banners bearing the very explicit message "Death to Israel". On several occasions, these provocations prompted the European military attachés in Tehran to leave the podium.[3]

In fact, for the first time since the birth of the State of Israel, another country in the region may not only have the will, but also be on the verge of having the capability to destroy it with non-conventional weapons. Tel Aviv can hardly ignore the situation, especially as, even if Iran is not foolhardy enough to attack Israel with a nuclear bomb, it is obvious that once Tehran has the bomb, the country's more radical elements will be bolstered. Iran would therefore probably be more aggressive and reckless in the entire region, with the means to wield a permanent threat over its potential enemies, including Israel. Finally, Israel is perfectly aware that there is the risk that other Middle Eastern countries might follow suit, thus making overall regional security even more volatile than it is today.

Israel's behaviour so far shows however that it prefers the diplomatic course and will support the European—or now P6—initiative for as long as there is hope of a negotiated solution. Israeli activity with regard to Iran consists therefore mainly of actively participating in the exchanges of information on Iran with all the key players—irrespective of whatever preparations the army may be making. Contrary to general belief, these exchanges are by no means confined to Washington. Since the beginning of the crisis in 2002-2003, Israel has maintained continual relations with Moscow, a crucial partner,[4] as well as with Paris, Berlin and London. These exchanges cover the development of the situation, the IAEA's discoveries and conclusions, and the strategies of the various actors. They enable Tel Aviv to stay informed of the analyses and intentions of the five capitals playing a key role in resolving the issue. Israel is aware of the ambiguities and even the contradictions of the Russian position, of America's dilemma as a result of domestic policy and the Iraq war, and, while it appreciates the trust the Europeans have continually demonstrated, it is conscious of the limits of their resolve should the situation deteriorate.

Naturally what everyone wants to know is whether Israel envisages military action if Russia's current diplomatic efforts fail, as they did in 2003 and 2004. This question actually has two parts: is a military operation technically feasible and would it be politically viable? Technically, even if it such an operation were a lot more difficult and risky than the bombing of Osirak in 1981,[5] the solutions exist provided the resources are there, particularly aircraft, and Israel may be prepared to embark on an intervention lasting several weeks. It would not be necessary to destroy all Iran's nuclear facilities, which are dispersed all over the country, but only the most critical ones, and other targets, for example the Iranian centres of power. To delay the programme would make sense if the objective is to keep nuclear weapons out of the hands of the current regime. The problem is rather that of the potential regional and internal consequences.

The international community remembers the Gulf War Coalition's anxiousness to convince Israel not to become involved in the conflict, even after Iraqi missiles had hit its capital. Tel Aviv agreed, recognising that its participation would be likely to transform the nature of the "Desert Storm" operation. An Israeli intervention against Iran, especially if successful, would probably make a lot of people happy, for nobody really has any idea how to resolve the problem. But who would dare admit it? Probably no one, especially in the region, but in Europe also. There should be no illusions on this point.

Israel is extremely conscious of this situation and would far prefer for the United States to take the initiative if it does come down to a military operation, especially in the run-up to the important elections of March 2006. The possibility of an Israeli intervention is unlikely unless Tel Aviv were to come to the triple conclusion that: one, the negotiation process had absolutely no chance of succeeding, two, Iran's nuclear programme was very close to a point of no return, and three, that Washington—which also has important elections in autumn 2006—would not run the risk of launching a new military operation.[6] After all, didn't Lieutenant Dan Halutz, Israel's military chief of staff, who was asked by foreign journalists in early December 2005 how far he was prepared to go to prevent Iran from acquiring the bomb, reply: "Two thousand kilometres"?

If it were to come to an Israeli intervention, it is likely that Iran would attack Israel, with either Shehab 3 missiles, renewed Hizbullah attacks on the north of Israel or terrorist attacks against Israeli interests and civilians outside Israel. Or it might use a combination of all three, over an indefinite period of time, if Israel were seen as the aggressor.

The risks are therefore huge. It is easy to understand why military intervention can only be considered as a last resort. The above explains why some observers talked about Israel's bombing of Hizbullah positions in Lebanon in July 2006 as a conflict with Iran. In a sense, it was.

9

NORTH KOREA: A ROLE MODEL?

Iran's relations with North Korea are one of the most disturbing aspects of its nuclear and ballistic missile programmes. In the 1980s, Pyongyang supported Iran against Saddam Hussein, supplying it with SCUD ballistic missiles, while Egypt helped Iraq in various ways (in addition to missiles, indications of a chemical weapons co-operation emerged, and it is possible that Egyptian experts were also involved in Iraq's biological weapons programme). The co-operation between North Korea and Iran became public in 1998 when experts noted the similarity between the Iranian Shehab 3 missiles and the North Korean No-Dong.[1] But North Korea may also have helped develop Iran's nuclear activities according to information—uncorroborated at this stage—often provided by Japanese newspapers. Furthermore, the United States regularly imposes sanctions on North Korean corporations for carrying out activities that contravene the Iran Non-Proliferation Act.[2]

1. *Ballistic missiles.* As mentioned above, North Korean assistance to Iran goes back to the 1980s, when it supplied Iran with missiles during the war against Iraq. These were chiefly SCUD C missiles with a range of 300 to 450 miles.[3] But it later provided longer-range (800 miles) No-Dong missiles, as the Shehab missiles test in 1998 revealed. Despite Tehran's repeated denials, this co-operation is now accepted

as an established fact by most experts, and it is currently suspected that North Korea is supplying technology related to missiles with a range of several thousand miles. For decades now, Iran has been constantly trying to increase the range of its ballistic missiles, which probably indicates that it is seeking to develop a strategic role that goes beyond the region. And North Korea, along with Russian and Ukrainian companies, is a major source of expertise and supply. In any case, this should give the Europeans, not only the Americans, some food for thought.

2. *Both countries have benefited from the Abdul Qadeer Khan network.* AQ Khan in person admitted as much in a written confession to the Pakistani authorities in Islamabad in 2004, and Iran eventually conceded it was true. North Korea, which may have a different view of its interests, continues to deny the charges. But its declarations do not carry much weight given the evidence now available to Western intelligence services. It has even transpired that planes lent by the United States to Islamabad to assist the fight against terrorism have been used to transport some of the nuclear-related equipment from Pakistan to North Korea. Furthermore, the existence of uranium conversion activities in North Korea was confirmed after the discovery of hexafluoride of North Korean origin in Libya in 2004.[4]

3. *Nuclear co-operation?* Several articles in the Japanese press, notably in the daily newspaper *Sankei Shimbun* in August 2003, have reported the presence of Iranian nuclear experts in North Korea over the last three years. Citing military sources, *Sankei Shimbun* alleged that there had been discussions between Tehran and Pyongyang on joint work related to nuclear warheads. In June 2004, the same newspaper claimed that North Korea and Iran were planning jointly to develop and test nuclear detonators. The article claimed that six Iranian experts had travelled to North Korea in May 2004, and that the trials were scheduled to take place between July and December 2004. In November 2004, the same source reported that North Korea had sold Iran several kilos of a key component for the production of uranium

hexafluoride. Tokyo never confirmed any of these assertions. Lastly, in July 2005, an article from the Japanese newspaper, picked up by the German daily *Die Welt*, reported that a large number of North Korean experts were now in Iran, that courses on sensitive nuclear topics were being run for handpicked Iranian scientists, and joint operations at a clandestine enrichment plant located between Isfahan and Shiraz were underway. These last claims were not verified, but several western embassies confirmed the presence of growing numbers of North Korean experts in Iran.

4. *A strategic partnership?* Some observers have pointed out that during the 2005 NPT Review Conference, Iran threatened to resume suspended activities at the same time as North Korea was threatening to proceed with nuclear tests. Both countries seem to have been well aware that managing two simultaneous crises would create a headache for Washington, especially given the US's ongoing military operations in Iraq. This does not mean that there is an alliance between Pyongyang and Tehran, but rather that a degree of tactical understanding is beneficial to both capitals. Iran has learned from Pyongyang's brinkmanship and handling of diplomatic relations with Western countries over more than a decade. As a result, common to both countries are contradictory declarations, sudden turnarounds, and a more conciliatory attitude before important deadlines followed by a renewed hardline stance. That said, Iran, with its known tendency to see itself as the centre of the Middle East, if not of the entire world, would hate to be compared to North Korea. Tehran uses Pyongyang, but it has only contempt for North Korea and has even made it known just how unjustified the comparison between the two countries would be. And yet, despite what the Iranians say, the confrontational stance adopted by President Ahmadinejad, his way of rejecting the Security Council demands and his recklessness are increasingly beginning to resemble the policy of Kim Jong-il.

Be that as it may, there still appears to be active co-operation between the two countries. Recently, according to several sources,

Iranians were again present at the North Korean missile tests on 5 July 2006 which were condemned on 15 July by the Security Council.

10

EGYPT: THE OPPORTUNITY TO
RETHINK ITS DEFENCE POLICY?

Egypt fears an Iranian nuclear bomb, which would be all the more worrying since Iran has never been an ally of the Arab countries in general or of Egypt in particular. But it is remarkable that this anxiety has never translated into the slightest action—not even diplomatic—from Cairo to support the European countries' efforts to negotiate with Iran prior to February 2006.[1] Worse, since 2004, Egypt's behaviour in multilateral disarmament and non-proliferation conferences has often played into the Iranians' hands on important issues. At the Third Preparatory Committee for the 2004 Review Conference of the Parties to the Treaty on the Non-Proliferation of Nuclear Weapons, Egypt's marked support enabled Tehran to block the consensus on the agenda for the Review Conference due to take place a year later.

Then, Egypt's policy was puzzling in a much more important context: the May 2005 NPT Review Conference itself. Egypt effectively helped Iran to emerge unscathed from a review exercise during which Tehran's violations should have been exposed, examined and condemned. No delegation had any idea what could be motivating the Egyptian diplomats and Cairo regime when the instructions were decided. Tehran benefited greatly from the Conference's failure to deal with any substantial work in New York in May 2005 and in particular to reach any decision related to Iran's withdrawal from the Treaty (article 10, 2 of the NPT). As a result, when and if Iran judges it appropriate, it can envisage following North Korea's example and withdraw from the NPT without suffering any serious consequences from this additional provocation. All requests to Cairo for explanations resulted in vehement, defensive replies that were not deemed convincing.

More than a year later, the following explanations could account for Egypt's attitude in May 2005:

— *An internal reason*. Cairo was going through a politically sensitive phase, with a resurgence of terrorism (Taba attacks in October 2004, Cairo in April 2005 and Sinai in June 2005), and the growing influence of the Muslim Brothers (later confirmed in the legislative elections in autumn 2005). The regime's organisational structures guaranteed President Mubarak a comfortable re-election in September 2005, but he may have felt it would be difficult to impose his son Gamal after this new mandate: the Egyptians were frustrated by the ongoing state of emergency, the economic situation and corruption among the elites. The announcement in February 2005 of a change to the Constitution to allow multiple candidatures and an election with universal suffrage did not fool many people: American pressure was becoming too strong and the concession was mainly superficial. Cairo—and therefore the Egyptian delegation to New York—may have wanted to demonstrate that Egypt was spearheading the opposition to the United States in the run-up to the political elections in the autumn. Furthermore, American pressure for the democratisation of the region was given a particularly cool reception in Cairo, Egypt being one of the most determined opponents of the notion of a "Greater Middle East". An expression of displeasure in New York is not unthinkable under these circumstances.

— *A security reason*. Many Egyptian diplomats have made it clear for years that the NPT no longer served Egypt's interests. No concession at all had ever been obtained from Israel; Pakistan (a non-Arab country) openly acquired a nuclear weapon in 1998; and, to crown everything, Iran was in the process of acquiring the bomb. Under these conditions, Egypt was probably wary of criticising two Muslim countries, but may however have considered that it should not cut off any of its options, including that of withdrawing from the NPT itself at some later stage. Tehran's regional ambitions are clear, both to Cairo and Riyadh, but Egypt may also have had in mind the additional problem of its rivalry with Saudi Arabia, a country Cairo might also suspect of seeking to acquire a nuclear bomb at some point, with the help of Pakistan, as a response to Tehran's ambitions.

— *Egypt and the Security Council.* The reform of the Security Council failed in 2005, but this was not yet apparent in May. If the enlargement of the Council had taken place in September 2005, the seat reserved for Africa in the reform would probably have gone either to South Africa or to Nigeria. Egypt's very visible policy in May could have stemmed from Cairo's wish to assert itself on the international stage, thus giving the impression that it was an essential presence in multilateral debates and bodies. That is similar to the strategy pursued by South Africa, with more assiduity and skill.

— *Egypt has carried out clandestine experiments.* The international community was somewhat surprised to learn in November 2004 that some small-scale conversion and reprocessing experiments took place in Egypt in the 1980s and 1990s (and even up until 2003), which had never been declared to the IAEA, and could be connected to activities that were not necessarily peaceful in nature. Notably, uranium metal had been imported and produced in Egypt, as well as a small quantity of almost weapon-grade high-enriched uranium. Uranium and thorium experiments were also conducted. The first discoveries were reportedly made by the IAEA in 2001, and one of the questions one might well ask is why it took the Vienna agency three years to launch a more in-depth investigation and communicate the results to the Board of Governors. Egyptian diplomats have constantly insisted on the limited scale of these undeclared activities, and justified these failures by invoking the incompetence and negligence of the technical managers. Be that as it may, Cairo is still refusing to sign the Additional Protocol to the IAEA Safeguards Agreement, which only adds weight to suspicions that the nuclear option is not completely closed. Questions had also been raised since December 2003 as to the level of knowledge that the Egyptian intelligence services had of Libya's clandestine nuclear programme which was being put into operation on Egypt's doorstep for twenty years.[2]

—— *Relations between Egypt and Iran remain dubious*. Relations between Egypt and Iran are tinged with suspicion, even hostility. But Cairo's conciliatory attitude forces us to ask whether the two capitals' *de facto* diplomatic convergence on the nuclear issue is purely coincidental and only tactical. Internal problems, external pressure and regional developments contribute to a possibly worrying shift in Cairo's diplomatic positions and defence policy, in which a rapprochement with Tehran is not inconceivable, even though it may mean "appeasement" more than anything else. After all, Cairo recently attempted to resume normal diplomatic relations. But if that was Egypt's objective, the new government in power in Iran since June 2005 is not likely to make things easy: the former mayor of Tehran is a great admirer of President Sadat's assassin!

11

SAUDI ARABIA: OPEN
RIVALRY IN THE GULF

Saudi Arabia has a long-standing tradition of hostility towards Iran. The rivalry between the two countries for the regional leadership became more intense in the 1980s and Iran has never forgiven Riyadh for supporting Baghdad during the Iran-Iraq war. However, the increased tensions between Saudi Arabia and Iraq at the end of the 1980s, and then the Gulf war, lessened the antagonism between Iran and Saudi Arabia. In the 1990s, under the presidency of Mohammed Khatami, top-level bilateral relations even led to a form of cordiality. The two countries also found common ground in the co-management of the oil market. In April 2001, they signed an agreement on regional security and in February 2002, Prince Abdullah openly repudiated the reference to Iran as part of the "axis of evil". But this still makes no difference to the fact that, for Riyadh, Tehran remains the sole serious external threat on the horizon, particularly with the rise of the Shia.

Unlike Egypt, Saudi Arabia took a clear and public stand against Iran's nuclear programme in 2005. And Riyadh tried to reassure the international community as to its own intentions by signing a safeguards agreement that same year.[1] Saudi Foreign Minister, Prince Saud al-Faysal bin Abdulaziz, declared in June 2005 that "the kingdom did not [possess] facilities, nuclear reactors or fissile materials" and that he was "anxious to co-operate continually with the IAEA" by pledging to abide by the NPT.

Saudi Arabia finally demonstrated clear support for the diplomatic talks between Iran and the Europeans during the Review Conference of the Non-Proliferation Treaty held in New York in May 2005. These initiatives may be due in part to Riyadh's wish for a rapprochement with Washington: relations have remained tense since the 9/11 attacks of 2001 because of the implication of a large number of Saudis. However, another influencing factor is certainly the fear that an open crisis with Iran, should the diplomatic process fail, would have repercussions for Saudi Arabia. In 2006, particularly after the events in Lebanon, this fear is naturally even more acute than it was in 2005.

Riyadh is also mindful of the experts' forecasts for the development of nuclear proliferation in the coming years, which regularly cite Saudi Arabia as a potential candidate. The reason lies in its close and longstanding relationship with Pakistan and the funding Riyadh has put into the Pakistani nuclear programme from the outset. It is bad enough to be linked to the worst terrorist attack in history without also being suspected of wanting to acquire the bomb with the aid of a country whose exploits on the clandestine nuclear market have been so much in the news! It is well known that relations between the Saudi and Pakistani intelligence services have been close for a long time, and Saudi officials have visited Pakistani military nuclear sites. Iran sought to exploit these suspicions by spreading the rumour in December 2004 that Pakistan and Saudi Arabia had signed an agreement by which Islamabad promised to help the kingdom develop nuclear weapons and acquire missiles that could give it superiority. The Iranian professor Abu Mohammed Asgarkani even stated at a conference that took place during this period that Iran's efforts to acquire a nuclear bomb had been stepped up when Tehran learned of this agreement. However, no confirmation has ever been given so far concerning such reports.

Saudi Arabia's efforts to calm down the speculation—or the suspicions—did not stop observers from keeping a close eye on its activities, particularly given the possibility that terrorists might steal nuclear materials or equipment. It was not enough to protest, claiming that "all radioactive products in Saudi Arabia are exclusively for the purpose of medical and petroleum research". True, the two phases of the Saudi nuclear programme—for this programme did indeed exist—were both halted after the accidents of Three Mile Island in the United States and Chernobyl in Ukraine. But this does not give a precise indication of what the Saudi Arabia will do once it is faced with the prospect of a nuclear Iran.

In Pakistan, the Saudis have close allies who can help them to acquire the bomb or cover up their efforts to acquire one. Riyadh has also shown an interest in nuclear-capable delivery systems. No one has forgotten that in the late 1980s Saudi Arabia secretly purchased some forty Chinese intermediate-range CSS2 missiles. Once this was known, there was strong pressure from Washington, which feared seeing these missiles with a range of 1,200 miles proliferate in the Middle East.

Since the invasion of Kuwait by Iraqi troops in 1990, Riyadh has become aware of its vulnerability. And after the invasion of Iraq by American troops in 2003, the political development of this country has become a major source of concern of a different order: the growing influence of Shia Islam in the region.[2] As regards Riyadh's position on this matter, the situation is pretty clear: Washington has created a mess in Iraq and should not pull out before fixing it.

Riyadh's lukewarm reaction to Israel's violent bombardment of Hizbullah positions in Lebanon in July and early August 2006 gives an insight into the level of fear felt by Saudi Arabia as Iran furthers its ambitions in the whole region.

12

SOUTH AFRICA: AN AMBIGUOUS PLAYER

The nuclear links between Iran and South Africa are complex and mystifying. They would appear to be of two kinds: commercial and diplomatic. But the possibility that South Africa has given Iran technical assistance with the fuel cycle cannot be ruled out, given the many visits to Iran by South African technicians and engineers between 2004 and 2005 (more than twenty according to Saudi sources). As it concerns part of the Iranian programme that can have either a civil or a military purpose, Pretoria could legitimately claim, if this information were officially confirmed after an investigation, that the assistance given was perfectly lawful. Besides, it is hard to see what interest South Africa could have in helping other countries develop nuclear weapons, having abandoned its own nuclear weapons programme. Only uncontrolled elements could in principle play this role.[1]

On the trade front, Iran is a major exporter of oil to South Africa (in particular since the resumption of diplomatic relations in 1994) and, as regards nuclear-related dealings, Tehran purchased large quantities of uranium from Pretoria in the 1980s: the declarations to the IAEA mention 485 tonnes of uranium concentrate, but one order of 1,500 tonnes is often referred to in other documents. Was all the uranium sold by South Africa to Iran during this period declared to Vienna? And were there not any subsequent sales by Pretoria, by the South

African establishment or via intermediaries? South Africa should be able to give answers to these questions.

The Iranians attempted to convince South Africa, one of the main non-aligned countries, to support Tehran's nuclear policy in the name of the "right to benefit from nuclear energy for peaceful purposes". Appealing to public opinion, the insistence on this right—which the NPT in no way confuses with a systematic right for a country to control on its soil the complete fuel cycle or even enrichment[2]—gained massive support in the developing countries. In August 2005, when there was an important vote by the IAEA Board of Governors in response to the resumption of conversion activities at Isfahan, Pretoria again put pressure on the Europeans to respect this "right". And South Africa has effectively maintained this stance, even after the formal recognition of Iran's violation of its non-proliferation commitments in September of the same year, and therefore its abuse of this "right".

And yet South Africa has excellent reasons to suspect Iran of having embarked on a nuclear military adventure, for it knows from experience the many methods of concealing a clandestine programme: Pretoria manufactured six nuclear missiles before abandoning its programme in 1991, when the end of apartheid seemed inevitable and President De Klerk decided to join the NPT as a non-nuclear power. The concealment methods used, which were disclosed in the 1990s, demonstrate great sophistication. Were some of these methods used by Tehran? In any case, South Africa is indisputably a country whose past experience, like its trade and diplomatic relations with Tehran, can be very useful for Iran's strategy.

And yet, as we have already pointed out, South Africa should be one of the countries most hostile to the acquisition of a nuclear weapon by a new country, since it dismantled its own programme. But the links between the two countries are still obviously close, and at times, unfathomable. For example, in 2005, South Africa agreed to examine an Iranian proposal to convert uranium concentrate at Iranian facilities and to export the hexafluoride thus produced for enrichment operations to be carried out in a third country. Note that this is very similar to the proposal put forward by Moscow in autumn 2005 which Tehran initially rejected, later to indicate that it could be considered. At some point, experts thought it was possible for this proposal to resurface if Iran, failing to strike a deal with Russia, were to decide to turn elsewhere. But this seems unlikely in 2006.

In September 2005, South Africa, which claimed to support the European strategy, again assisted Iran by announcing its hostility to the referral of the Iranian nuclear dossier to the Security Council. Then, shortly afterwards, a delegation including Cuba, South Africa and Malaysia travelled to Tehran to reaffirm the right of signatories to the NPT to benefit from nuclear energy for peaceful purposes. Likewise, in February 2006, when a resolution to refer Iran to the Security Council was adopted with the backing of twenty-seven states including India, Egypt and Brazil, South Africa chose to abstain. And yet, Pretoria had once more assured the Europeans of its support just before voting took place. There are definitely some ambiguous factors in the relations between Iran and South Africa.

13

THE IAEA: NO REFERRAL TO
THE SECURITY COUNCIL

The IAEA is playing for high stakes in Iran. It does not want a repeat of the criticisms it received in 1991 for not having uncovered Iraq's nuclear programme, even though when the Gulf War broke out it was at a highly advanced stage on every front and reportedly Iran was only a few months away from the development of a nuclear device, using materials under international safeguards.

The very first problem for the IAEA is that it did not uncover the Iranian programme for eighteen years. Iran's post-revolution clandestine nuclear activities go back to 1985, on its own admission. But it was only possible to convince the IAEA of the need for a thorough investigation into Iran's activities after the press conference held in Washington by the Iranian opposition in exile in summer 2002. Vienna never considered the information available prior to that announcement sufficient to launch intrusive inspections on Iranian soil. Furthermore, the inspections only began in February 2003, after months of delays. Since then, the incriminating evidence—and the suspicions of the international community—have only mounted. The internal tensions at the IAEA over the handling of this case, as well as over the content of the reports made to the Board of Governors, have attracted comment in several capitals. In the crucial period between

2003 and 2005, the Director General, Mohammed ElBaradei, was manifestly more accommodating towards Tehran than the former Head of Safeguards, Pierre Goldschmidt, who left the position at the end of June 2005.[1] Mohammed ElBaradei's judgement was constantly political, while his predecessor, as well as the Director of Safeguards, had kept to the Agency's core mission, which is of a technical nature. The only non-proliferation political authority must remain the Security Council.

On his departure from the IAEA, Pierre Goldschmidt gave an interview[2] in which he clearly emphasised Iran's lack of co-operation with the IAEA over the major unresolved questions:[3] enriched uranium contamination and works carried out on P2 centrifuges based on blueprints supplied in 1995 by Pakistan. This situation has little chance of improving with the new Iranian president, and, as the IAEA's former Head of Safeguards again wrote, the world was already caught up in "a race against time" with Iran before Ahmadinejad's arrival in power. In this race, the IAEA had a crucial role: to elucidate all the unresolved questions and conduct the necessary investigations to reach the credible conclusion that there are no undeclared materials in Iran and no clandestine nuclear programme. In such a vast country, that is no easy matter. But if the Nobel peace prize was awarded to the IAEA and its director in autumn 2005, in all likelihood it was to encourage the Agency to embark on this task with determination.

— *The only multilateral agency.* The IAEA is in a unique position: what the inspectors report to the Agency's secretariat and what the secretariat reports to the Board of Governors is widely accepted as "objective" and not distorted by any interest, national or otherwise. It remains to be established whether this is true in the case of Iran, and if the Agency has really done everything within its power to prevent the development of an Iranian nuclear bomb. For there are certainly conflicting opinions within the Agency on this question, which are apparent in its reports. These sometimes contain contradictory, or at least hardly compatible, assessments. For example, the report submitted to the Board of Governors in November 2003 contains a long list of Iran's failures to meet its obligations and mentions "a policy of concealment". But these words are immediately toned down by the only sentence that the press picked up on: "To date, there is no evidence that the previously undeclared nuclear material and activities referred to above were related to a nuclear weapons programme." Naturally, these words were abundantly cited by Tehran. The Agency, at the very highest level, has had, and still has, some strange reservations about referring the case to the Security Council, whatever the nature of the discoveries made on the ground, whereas it should remain neutral on the issue.[4] Furthermore, since there is no real expertise on nuclear weapons development within the IAEA, or very little, the work done in this respect comes up against obvious limitations. In the case of Iran, which may be in possession of a weapon design supplied by the AQ Khan network, this deficiency poses a problem, especially when it comes to evaluating the information submitted to the IAEA by Washington, London, Paris and Berlin. An article in the *Wall Street Journal* of 27 July 2005 by Carla Anne Robbins effectively pointed out that the intelligence services of these countries had briefed the IAEA on an important dossier in Farsi, which apparently described the warhead's characteristics in detail, from which it could be inferred that Iran has actively worked on developing a nuclear bomb. This information has never been refuted by any of the five actors in question. But the IAEA never seemed to accord it any particular attention and it did not change the cautious and bureaucratic style of its reports from which it is very difficult to come to a precise view concerning the nature of the programme. Lastly, there are factual errors in the IAEA reports: that of February 2004, for example, confuses first-generation Iranian P1 centrifuges and Libyan L1 centrifuges with G1 centrifuges, a much less complex German model than the Dutch model on which the Iranian and Libyan types are built. This confusion raised unhelpful doubts as to the Agency's competence. George Perkovich, a renowned expert on non-proliferation issues, voiced his fear that the IAEA had become hyper cautious on a political basis in an open letter to the Director General of the IAEA in 2005: "Many capitals are so resistant to the current administration's bullying that they urge you to cook the books to produce reports that will forestall another Iraq-style showdown."[5]

The Agency's neutrality, its ability to confine itself to the facts and to report these facts, or rather all the facts, to the Board of Governors must be beyond criticism. Hence one might wonder why, in February and in June 2005, Mohammed ElBaradei decided not to produce any written report on Iran. It was not for lack of news at that time,[6] and the decision to restrict the Director of Safeguards to making a verbal report was debatable. Before the June 2005 meeting, and the Iranian elections, the IAEA thought it was advisable to keep a low profile to avoid playing into the hands of the most conservative elements in Tehran. As the result of the presidential elections showed, this was not a sound argument: the attitude of the Vienna Agency played no role at all in the process. But the absence of a written report was interpreted by Tehran as a "softening" of the Agency's stance and an additional sign of weakness.

—— *IAEA however has a difficult relationship with Iran.* The history of relations between the IAEA and Iran is full of cover-ups, major delays in giving the international inspectors access to the sites,[7] and attempts to impede or restrict the inspections. An interesting illustration of the way the two parties behave towards each other is the inspection of the Parchin complex which took place on 12 January 2005. The IAEA had been interested in this facility for several months. Missiles and powerful explosives are produced there and there was a suspicion that "cold testing" (without nuclear materials) had been carried out, as well as other clandestine nuclear activities. This type of testing, for which there can be no possible justification in a civil nuclear energy programme, would constitute a blatant proof that Iran has a nuclear weapons programme. When the inspection finally took place in January 2005, the IAEA was only authorised to visit one of the four areas it was interested in, and, in this one area, was only allowed access to a limited number of buildings. Furthermore, the environmental samples produced no results as these too were restricted to certain areas. Iran's lack of co-operation is blatant in this instance, but the reasons why the IAEA agreed to work under such unsatisfactory conditions also raise disturbing questions. Why did the IAEA not make full use of its rights, in particular those conferred on it by the Additional Protocol?[8]

The most striking feature of the IAEA's behaviour, if we exclude the mass of new information gathered about Iran's activities, is the institution's reluctance to recognise Iran's patent violations. All sorts of euphemisms and understatements were used in the reports and it was not until September 2005 that Iran was declared to be unequivocally in violation of its obligations in a Board of Governors resolution which cites article 12 of the IAEA statutes, making it compulsory for a report to be submitted to the Security Council. There could be a number of explanations for the IAEA's stalling, which can have serious consequences with regard to a country in a hurry to acquire a nuclear bomb: the risk of being barred access to Iranian territory, the fear of losing control of a case that could move from a technical to a political level, and the sense that a situation akin to that of Iraq might develop. But none of these explanations must disguise the fact that it is not the IAEA's job to make judgements of this nature, otherwise it will lose the very thing that earned it a Nobel Prize for international peace and security: its neutrality.

— *The IAEA tentatively supported the Europeans' initiative*. In October 2003, the relationship between the IAEA and Iran being in an impasse due to Tehran's refusal to comply with a Board of Governors resolution, the Vienna Agency gave a frosty reception to the announcement of an agreement between Tehran and the European troika, despite the detailed information submitted by Paris, London and Berlin to the Director General of the IAEA at every stage of the negotiations, and the fact that the Europeans were "bailing out" the IAEA. After the signing of the Agreement, the IAEA sought to limit the "scope" of the agreed suspension on the grounds that it was too extensive to be compatible with the Agency's status. The problem of the scope of the Agreement was therefore the subject of lengthy prevarication between October 2003 and February 2004. This proved ineffective, even damaging, for at the second negotiation, the field of suspended activities had to be widened to include uranium conversion. Furthermore, despite the support obtained by the Europeans from their colleagues on the Board of Governors, the IAEA never declared its position on whether the "suspension" agreed with the Europeans should be upheld or lifted. This suspension was always considered "voluntary", and could therefore be called into question at any time. This has led to some serious problems, given that the IAEA is the ultimate nuclear non-proliferation authority. When for example, Iran carried out tests on centrifuge components in January 2005, these were judged to be in contravention of the commitments made to the Europeans on 15 November 2004; but in his February report to the Board, the Head of Safeguards, mindful of the Agency's status and not the agreement between the European Union and Iran, did not cite them as a lapse. Consequently, there has always been a gap between the Europeans and the IAEA which Iran has been able to exploit to its advantage. In more general terms, the IAEA has never doubted that the nuclear programme embarked on by Iran has no economic justification and that it has a military objective. But there has been no declaration to this effect by the Agency. Often, the IAEA reports do not make it possible to grasp the evolution of the situation. What conclusion is to be drawn, for example, from a sentence such as this: "The Director General noted an increased degree of co-operation by Iran, while noting that some of the information and access were at times slow in coming and incremental, and that some of the information was in contrast to that previously provided by Iran"?[9] Are we meant to understand that Iran is co-operating, that Iran provides information late? That it is delaying the inspectors on some sites by not allowing them immediate access? That it changes its declarations? Frankly, it is hard to tell. In the November 2004 report to the Board of Governors, a long list of Iran's failures to meet its obligations is given in paragraph 86, but the following phrase, already cited concerning the November 2003 report, is curiously inserted in the same document: "To date, there is no evidence that the previously undeclared nuclear material and activities referred to above were related to a nuclear weapons programme." So what could be the meaning of Iran's secrecy over two decades, of its uranium metal conversion activities, of its many attempts to acquire beryllium, of its polonium 210 production and its conflicting declarations? Be that as it may, these words having been written, the IAEA has to demonstrate to the international community that it really has done everything within its power to justify this assertion. To do so, it should have made uncompromising use of all its rights under the Additional Protocol. That is one of the reasons why the report of 3 September 2005 demands increased powers to enable the inspectors to fulfil their remit (paragraph 50). The Security Council would be the best placed to respond to that demand. But whether the case is submitted, not for information but for action, is another matter.

And it is also necessary for the IAEA's Iran inspectors to be able to get on with their job. But two inspectors have been removed, Jhon Hi Li and Chris Charlier, not for professional misconduct, but on the contrary, because of their efficiency, at the request of Tehran.[10] Who is giving orders to the Agency? The Board of Governors or the country under examination?

CONCLUSION

I The main questions

1. *What does Iran want?* Despite all of Tehran's talk of the peaceful purposes of its nuclear programme, the answer to this question is straightforward. Iran wants the bomb. But it would like to acquire it while preserving international respectability, avoiding UN sanctions and developing its economy (essential to provide employment for young people, who make up 70% of the population). Even in 2006, Iran is not yet entirely convinced that it cannot hold on to these four advantages at the same time.[1] The rest of the world is more sceptical, especially since Mahmoud Ahmadinejad's arrival in power, even if the question of actual sanctions is a sensitive one.[2] And yet this goes to the heart of the collective security system, and there is a danger for the United Nations of a gradual return to the impotence of the Society of Nations if the violation of agreements as important as the NPT does not lead to any kind of sanctions.

2. *What level of enrichment has Iran already achieved?* According to the Iranians, their scientists and technicians had never gone beyond the threshold of 1.2% before April 2006 when Tehran declared that the level of 3.5 had been reached. But traces of uranium enriched to more than 70% and 54% and 36% were found in samples taken from the Kalaye electric plant, where most of the enrichment efforts between

95

1995 and 2003 took place. At Natanz, further traces of uranium enriched to 54% were also found, as well as on other sites. Iran claims
that all traces of uranium over 1.2% are due to contamination from
imported equipment. That may be true for some pieces imported
from Pakistan, but it is impossible to prove unless the inspectors have
access to the Pakistani facilities. As Islamabad refuses to grant this, the
components it supplied to the IAEA after prolonged delays can just as
well have come from Iran.

3. *Why does Iran want to continue with conversion activities?* The haste with
which the Isfahan plant started up again on 8 August 2005 underscores
the pertinence of this question. The purpose of the plant is to produce
UF_6, the pre-enrichment stage. This gas must be of high quality and
Iran is said to have experienced difficulties achieving this in the past. It
seems however to have overcome them, perhaps with outside help. If
enrichment is not permitted subsequent to this conversion, producing
UF_6 is pointless, unless clandestine enrichment facilities do exist at
a site other than Natanz. Some experts support small-scale conversion and enrichment in Iran. This is a ludicrous position, given that a
small-scale plant can have no civil purpose: the quantities of enriched
uranium would be much too limited, but such activities could either
provide useful training or be replicated at a clandestine military site.
For the time being, neither the Europeans, nor the Americans, nor
the Russians are prepared to accept this proposal. At the Munich Conference on Security Policy of February 2005, the Defence Minister,
Sergei Ivanov, in response to a question, indicated that Moscow would
authorise neither conversion nor enrichment on Iranian soil.

4. *Is Iran on the point of possessing the necessary quantity of UF_6 to produce
a nuclear bomb?* In August 2006, as this book goes to press, without
a shadow of a doubt as far as quantity is concerned, but questions
remain as to the purity of the product. Tens of tonnes of uranium
concentrate have been converted to UF_4 and then to UF_6 since August
2005. More than 100 tonnes of UF6 are now available in Iran. This
is a capital question, for the resumption of conversion activities in

August 2005 was to enable Iran to cross a decisive threshold very quickly. Effectively, once the Isfahan conversion facility was up and running again, the time required to convert the 27 to 30 tonnes of UF_4 to UF_6 was estimated at just over a month, in other words, much less time that it took the Board of Governors and the Security Council to make a decision. This quantity is sufficient to obtain, after enrichment, enough materials for several nuclear bombs, hence the need to remove these materials from Iran as quickly as possible. There were several conversion campaigns between August and December 2005, and by early 2006, Iran was in possession of at least 85 tonnes of UF_6 (that is the quantity produced since September 2005 according to the IAEA report of February 2006), and 110 tonnes in May. This material is stored in tunnels protecting it from potential bomb attacks. One of the crucial problems concerns the later stage and the ignorance surrounding Iranian activities conducted on military sites, particularly with regard to the so-called P2 centrifuge which is much more efficient than the P1 used at Natanz and whose history since the acquisition of the blueprints in 1995 has never been clarified by the IAEA.

5. *What would the capacity of the Natanz enrichment facility be if it were used to produce nuclear weapons?* According to the Iranians, by the time construction is completed, this plant should house 54,000 P1 centrifuges. It could produce around 600 kilos of 93% enriched uranium a year. This is the equivalent of some twenty nuclear bombs. But it would take several years to build the 54,000 centrifuges. On the other hand, the rapid assembly of 3,000 machines is feasible. In this case, the annual production capacity would certainly be much lower, but sufficient however to produce one or two devices a year. The figure of 3,000 centrifuges has often been cited by the Iranian negotiators and there are sufficient components available at Natanz to assemble approximately this number. This of course does not take into account the possible existence of other and more efficient centrifuges at other facilities. Over time, these could become the main source of con-

cern, if Natanz progressively becomes a mere window dressing for
the IAEA.

6. *What is the real significance for the development of Iran's weapons programme of the suspension obtained by the Europeans between 2003 and 2005?*
The problem with this question is that we do not know for sure how
advanced the work carried out on the various civil and military sites
is. By definition, since the suspension was confined to conversion
(November 2004 to August 2005) and enrichment and reprocessing
related activities (October 2003 to August 2005 with some interrup-
tion), it did not hinder any other activity necessary to acquiring the
nuclear bomb. What the agreements signed in 2003 and 2004 with the
Europeans sought to block was access to fissile materials. They did not
relate to work on explosives or on improving warhead design. As far
as delivery systems are concerned, Iran is in the process of acquiring a
two-stage missile, with a potential range of 1,200 miles which could
be improved further. In the best-case scenario, Iran's programme has
somehow been delayed because it does not have access to some means
of production of nuclear materials (conversion and enrichment). In
the worst case, the suspension will have enabled Iran to avoid the
Security Council during a crucial period while it improved the efficiency of its technology. In a July 2005 interview, Dr Hassan Rohani,
the chief Iranian negotiator under President Khatami, stated that the
Isfahan facility project had not been suspended "for a moment until
the project was completed and tested and its product was achieved.[3]
The Arak project was never suspended either", and "today, we have
a considerable number of completed and ready to use centrifuges".
He concludes: "If we want to have a comparison in technical and legal
aspects between our conditions at the present time and at the beginning of the crisis, I think no one can deny that we have made very
significant progress since then."[4] In fact, after having overestimated
Iraqi capabilities in 2002 and 2003, we run the risk of underestimating
those of Iran, just as Iraqi capabilities were underestimated in 1990. It
now seems that most of the elements of a military programme are in

place, including the requirements for the reduction of UF_6 to metal, the casting and machining of uranium metal into hemispherical forms and the adaptation of the delivery vehicle to a nuclear warhead. Assuming that the first significant quantity (25kg according to the IAEA) can be produced within a year by a 3000 centrifuge plant of the P1 type, this plant could be terminated by 2007 and the 25 kg produced by 2008. If more sophisticated centrifuges of the P2 type (four times faster) have been assembled in some undisclosed location—as Mahmoud Ahmanidejad suggested in mid-April—the possibility that Iran will soon be able to produce a sufficient quantity of high-enriched uranium is even greater.

7. *What can the Security Council do?* One of the most remarkable characteristics of the debate is the fact that those who in principle support multilateralism have also been the most reluctant to call upon the Security Council to deal with a case that should have been referred in November 2003, if the statutes of the IAEA (article 12) had been applied immediately by the Board of Governors. The fear of coming to a decision was "justified" by the other fear that the Security Council will prove impotent and "unable to do anything" if the Iran case is referred to it. This is of course erroneous. The Council has a whole array of possible measures at its disposal. It can adopt a staged plan, the first phase of which would consist of making the suspension mandatory, including the construction of the Arak reactor able to produce plutonium (this is what Resolution 1696 contains), demanding that all materials produced since August 2005 be removed from Iran and giving the international inspectors increased rights of access to sites, documents and individuals (those two measures are still to be decided). Convincing explanations concerning the past activities of Lavizan-Shian should be obtained, the managers of the Gchine uranium mine interviewed and comprehensive information on the P2 centrifuges, enriched uranium contamination and on the laser enrichment programme provided. If Iran co-operates with these initial requests, it will be possible to resolve the case without further,

more damaging, economic measures being applied. During this period however, deliveries of Russian fuel should continue to be suspended. If these measures are not implemented, sanctions could be imposed as a second stage, beginning with a freeze on arms imports and a ban on investment in oil and gas infrastructure. An embargo on oil could be proposed at a later stage, taking account of the fact that Iran's need to sell its oil and gas is at least as great, if not greater than the rest of the world's need to purchase it. And finally, at the end of the process, as a matter of principle, no measures should be ruled out from the start, not even the use of force, if Iran refuses to comply. It should be noted that in the interview given by Hassan Rohani in July 2005 quoted above, the Iranian negotiator underlines that even before the matter was transferred to the UNSC, some economic consequences were noticeable in Iran. Speaking about the situation after September 2003, when there were already noises being made about the possible referral to New York, he said: "Almost all of Iran's economic activities were blocked. A decline in business activities pervaded the entire market and even ordinary trades were affected, because they had publicised to the world that Iran's case was going to the Security Council after the elapse of the deadline."

8. *Who is benefiting from the delays?* Here, the answer should be brief because there is no question: the delays are in Iran's favour. All concerned should bear this in mind.

II The scenarios

1. *The pursuit of the Iranian game.* The Iranian negotiators have continually reiterated their determination to pursue their nuclear activities on their territory while seeking to avoid a reaction to the repeated violations noted by the IAEA and the Security Council. This was their motive in using the negotiations with the Europeans. Talks were sought by Tehran at crucial moments when Iran's case was likely to be referred to the Security Council, i.e. in October 2003, November 2004, and then (with Russia) from September 2005 to February

2005. As of the summer of 2006, the situation is not sufficiently clear, since no Security Council action is expected before September and events in Lebanon are obviously a complicating factor. Iran knows that the Security Council remains divided on further action and that neither the Americans nor the Europeans have a proper strategy. As regards the United States, the lack of direction is palpable, and, as for the European countries, past experience speaks volumes. In September 2005, they did not carry out their threat to refer the case to the Security Council despite the resumption of conversion activities and a clear majority at the Board of Governors; in October 2005, the Europeans seemed ready to accept the resumption of conversion activities; and the decision to restart enrichment in January 2006 has still not produced any decisive results other than a UNSC resolution in July. The main challenge in 2006 is for Iran to continue its enrichment and conversion activities as well as to complete the Arak heavy water production plant without the Security Council taking action.

2. *A new phase of negotiations.* Once negotiations begin, they are hard to stop, both because the negotiators get hooked and because neither side wants to accept responsibility for failure. The negotiations which culminated in the European proposals of summer 2005, made public after the investiture of the new Iranian president, had been going on since December 2004, but these already represent a second stage, the first agreement dating back to 21 October 2003. After August 2005, it became increasingly clear that Iran had appointed a ruling power that would not back down and was probably there precisely to fulfil that role. The main question facing the international community is whether it will continue to accept the policy of the *fait accompli*, thus losing all credibility regarding the respecting of treaties, or start a third round of negotiations with little hope of being any more successful (the P6 offer) or finally start imposing incremental sanctions. The Europeans—and the Americans—would gladly opt for the second route, content to embark on a third round of negotiations with Russia, but Iran can also choose confrontation. The crisis of July

2006 triggered by Hizbullah erupted just as Moscow was prepared to support a declaration by the five permanent members and Germany asking for the Iranian dossier to go back to the Security Council, a few days before the G8 Summit in St Petersburg. And a month later, Iran proposed a new round of negotiations that could result—at the end of the process—in another suspension, completely changing the priorities set by the six powers in June.

3. *An agreement with the Russians.* At the beginning of 2006, the main achievement after two years of negotiations with the three European capitals was for the Iranian case to end up temporarily in the hands of Moscow! The Russians quickly found themselves faced with the same dilemma as the Europeans before them. Tehran will not back down except under very strong pressure, which can only come from a joint action of the Five in New York, but they wanted to play the mediators and attempted the impossible, in other words to convince Mahmoud Ahmadinejad and Ayatollah Khamenei to renounce willingly a programme that has been going on for twenty years. By the end of July 2006, Moscow's chief preoccupation still seemed to be to gain time, just like Tehran.

4. *The IAEA finds proof of prohibited activities in Iran.* Each Board of Governors meeting is the opportunity for additional disclosures and it is not impossible that there will be further findings incriminating Iran. Iran has shown its ability to conceal large facilities for very long periods of time. But it is hard to see—apart perhaps from a clandestine P2 pilot plant—what could be more decisive that the information gathered to date. The problem is not that of technically analysing Iran's activities, on which there is widespread agreement despite the public declarations, it is that of the will to respond to these activities. And there, the situation is far from brilliant.

5. *Security Council action.* In the event that Resolution 1696 is not implemented, the Security Council has a range of options at its disposal before envisaging sanctions or military action. The only sanctions that could seriously affect Iran are those relating to the oil and gas

industries. An oil or gas embargo looks highly unlikely, in view of its international consequences (drop in oil supply) and internal repercussions (effects on the Iranian population).[5] But an embargo on refined products widely imported by Iran would have an immediate impact. There are already problems with petrol in Iran and Mahmoud Ahmadinejad is far from being able to fulfil his campaign promises. At the beginning of 2006, Tehran had to consider petrol rationing without any sanctions having been imposed on the country. The reason is that consumers pay less than six times the real price because the government subsidises petrol. Drivers used 67 millions litres a day in 2005, and they are expected to use 73 million in 2006. Iran may be a major oil exporter, but it cannot meet domestic demand: 40% is refined abroad. There may well be a public backlash on this front. Furthermore, given the state of Iran's infrastructure in both cases, the lack of foreign investment in these sectors would have a huge effect and should also be considered as an option. Iran is particularly interested in Western investment, the Asian companies (China and India) having nothing like the same level of technical performance. Without these investments, Iran's production is almost guaranteed to decline, whereas in fact its output needs to increase. The two sectors would only be able to achieve this growth with new investments and improved management. Iran's 1979 level of production has still not been equalled in 2006. The additional advantage of an embargo on investments in oil and gas is that it would not have any effects on the global supply for about ten years and its impact on the price of oil could be controlled. And lastly, it offers greater flexibility than an embargo on oil and gas. However, it is unreasonable to discard the latter option purely and simply out of hand: the question is, does an Iranian nuclear bomb pose a sufficient security problem to take that type of risk. Furthermore, if an Iranian bomb could prompt Riyadh to reconsider its own non-proliferation commitments, it is not hard to imagine what the price of crude oil could be in the future if Iran's ambitions are not contained! As a result of not thinking about the future, one ends up with unsound reasoning. Lastly, faced with this sort of pressure, the main players in Tehran could well end up divided over the price to pay for a bomb that would bring few obvious advantages whereas the disadvantages are becoming increasingly evident (Arab neighbours reviewing their defence options, international isolation, inability to guarantee the economic development Iran needs to meet the growing employment demand). But this possibility must be examined taking account of the fact that the Iranian regime in power is prepared to go a long way in the confrontation and that fear is growing within the country and abroad.

6. *Military action.* The American administration has never ruled out any option for resolving the Iranian problem, including the use of force. Some experts believe that an Iranian crisis similar to the Cuban missile crisis will eventually become inevitable if the problem is not resolved before Iran acquires the bomb. But it is obvious that this option is not favoured by Washington because of the considerable difficulties involved.

First of all, the violence in Iraq and the fact that the American presence will be maintained there longer than anticipated; secondly Iran's damage capability, not only in Iraq but also in Afghanistan, Israel and Lebanon; thirdly, a crisis can erupt at any point in North Korea, and some senior American officials believe that the Far East may be even more worrying than the Middle East; fourthly, the difficulty the president of the United States will have in explaining his decision to Congress. Lastly, the USA knows that it would probably be alone in this operation, and that it cannot count on the support of any European capital. That said, preparations are doubtless being made. In January 2005, there were countless rumours about American reconnaissance missions in Iran to prepare for possible strikes.[6] The USA would prefer to see an Israeli action against Iran, but Tel Aviv also considers that such a decision is very risky and would rather see an American initiative. These two protagonists have not had their final say, especially if they come to the conclusion that the point of no return is getting close and that the future must not be sacrificed to the present.

On the Iranian side, several military scenarios are thought to have been examined: air attacks on the nuclear facilities, more ambitious air attacks on the centres of power, land intervention confined to special forces action, land invasion. Iran is acquiring large stocks of weapons, notably from Russia, even in 2006, and is building up to an asymmetrical war and guerrilla actions. Its reported use of Hizbullah in summer 2006 may be a taste of things to come.

III The lessons to be learned

There are many lessons to be learned from the Iranian nuclear case:

— *On the demands of the international community concerning the "evidence" of a violation of the treaties.* What exactly would constitute "evidence" of this kind acceptable to all concerned is hard to tell. In truth it is difficult, other than to wait for a nuclear test of the type carried out by India and Pakistan in 1998, to obtain a greater number of indicators of a nuclear weapons programme than in the case of Iran: a decision to resume its nuclear programme in 1985, in the midst of the war against Iraq, twenty years of concealment from the IAEA, multiple linkages of the nuclear programme to the military, inexplicable purchasing attempts related to a civil nuclear energy programme, activities blatantly connected to weapons development (production of uranium metal, polonium 210 and beryllium), constantly changing explanations according to the inspectors' findings, the destruction of evidence and the demolition of buildings before inspection, refusing access to the sites when requested (Lavizan and Parchin), to key information (location of the P2 centrifuges) and to personnel holding crucial information for the investigation (managers of the Physics Research Centre, the Gchine uranium mine and the laser enrichment programme). Added to all this is the withholding of documents indicating the method for casting and machining uranium metal into hemispheres. However, since November 2003, it has not been possible to obtain action by the United Nations Security Council.

— *On the role of the fuel cycle in the development of nuclear weapons.* The Iranian case has provided the opportunity to rethink the question of access to enrichment and reprocessing, particularly by countries of concern and which have no economic justification for developing an autonomous fuel cycle. This is the case of Iran which, over the months and years, has in fact almost given up providing justifications on this point. Several proposals have emerged as a result of this experience, some suggesting quite simply the universal halting of any further enrichment or reprocessing activities in any new country for a given period; others envisage a guarantee that fuel for countries under international suspicion will only come from outside sources (either supplied by a country or a regional consortium). The Review Conference of the Parties to the Treaty on the Non-Proliferation of Nuclear Weapons could have been the occasion to examine the options, but it did not reach any substantial conclusion. Discussions on this issue are to continue.

— *On the American and the European perspectives regarding the fight against proliferation.* Both camps have had to move closer to the other's viewpoint and adopt less clear-cut views on the value of international treaties and organisations. The Americans had to acknowledge that the IAEA inspectors have succeeded in gathering much more extensive and complete information on the ground than that previously provided by the intelligence services. Furthermore, allowing Iran to remain within the NPT is essential in order for these international inspections to continue. Meanwhile, for the Europeans it has become increasingly clear that additional non-proliferation initiatives are vital, like the Proliferation Security Initiative (PSI) for example, which makes it possible to intercept ships, planes or land transports when they are suspected of carrying equipment or materials that could be used for a clandestine non-conventional weapons programme. It also has to be accepted that the IAEA is not an entirely neutral interlocutor, especially when it is a matter of reporting *all* the facts related to violations. For both America and Europe, it has become obvious that negotiations that are not accompanied by any threat in the event of a failure to meet obligations have no chance of success. But since the Iranian elections, the two sides of the Atlantic have perhaps tended to be divided anew, despite agreeing on the surface: after having granted excessive importance to the expected but not realised election of Rafsanjani, the Europeans tend to act as though the unexpected arrival of an ultra-conservative president has not changed much. And yet one of the first results was the end of negotiations between Iran and the European troika and the beginning of a very disturbing political rhetoric. The key thing for Iran is visibly to gain time and to move forward on its weapons programme. On the American side, caution has given way to a very evident distrust of Tehran, especially since autumn 2005, but US policy has still moved towards possible talks with Tehran in July 2006 in the event that the suspension of fuel cycle activities were to be accepted by Tehran. Autumn 2006 will shed further light on the next steps to be adopted, taking into account the Lebanon crisis as a major warning.

— *On some broader issues.* Could the NPT survive another major crisis after the withdrawal of North Korea in January 2003? That is the question. And if the UNSC is unable to impose its will in this crisis, this will also have a major impact on global governance, which is already in bad shape. The outcome of the Iranian crisis can therefore have widespread consequences—and not only for the non-proliferation regime. Regionally, the consequences could be disastrous. If the Iranian nuclear question were a matter of a developing country wanting to obtain a symbol of power, it would still be worrying, but it could be viewed as no more serious than the acquisition of the bomb by India in 1974. But that is not the only issue at stake. In fact, the entire strategic order of the Middle East and the Gulf, an already highly volatile region, could be altered by the appearance of an Iranian nuclear bomb. If several players who are wary of each other were to acquire a nuclear capability, the risk of an uncontrollable situation developing is considerable. The conditions for an effective deterrent, always delicate in any case, especially when there are a number of players involved, would hardly be fulfilled. The crisis of summer 2006 brings with it new factors reinforcing this, as if there were any need. In the longer term, Iran could become a major factor in the event of a crisis in the Far East over Taiwan, given the close ties between Iran and China. But nobody is talking about that, and few are even considering the subject. And globally, what Iran is about to show is that there is no longer anyone in control of the international scene.

NOTES

INTRODUCTION

1 A view upheld throughout the electoral period, against all reason, since the Iranian negotiators left little doubt as to Tehran's intentions of resuming uranium conversion and enrichment, whatever the outcome of the elections.

2 This action was quite rightly seen as an important stage of the process begun in autumn 2002. But, in submitting all the International Atomic Energy Agency's resolutions to the Security Council, the Board of Governors stated that no action by the Council should be instigated before March, which gave Iran an extra month's leeway.

3 For example, an embargo on refined petroleum products, which are very extensively imported by Iran and whose consumption is rapidly growing, would have an immediate impact on the Iranian population. The regime appears to be much more sensitive to this internal pressure than to any external pressure.

4 By the end of March 2006, it appeared that the rate of assembly of Iranian centrifuges on the Natanz site exceeded forecasts. But it did slow down in summer 2006, and questions were then raised concerning the possible assembly of Iranian centrifuges at a clandestine site unknown to international inspectors.

1. IRAN: INDISPUTABLE MILITARY NUCLEAR AMBITIONS

1 In fact, it was two days before the investiture of the new president on 3 August that Iran officially informed the IAEA of its intention to resume

conversion activities at Isfahan. The crisis therefore began even before Ahmadinejad officially assumed power.

2   The Pasdaran are also known as the Islamic Revolutionary Guard Corps and the Bassiji are militiamen in civilian clothes. They are the main supporters of the regime up and down the country.

3   This does not mean that Mahmoud Ahmadinejad did not enjoy popular support thanks to his economic promises and the blatant corruption of the other candidates. But the fact is that nobody outside Tehran knew him before the elections.

4   The main Iraqi supporter of Iranian policy is Moqtada el Sadr.

5   The demonstrations in Lebanon in February 2006 over the Danish cartoons of the Prophet which had appeared four months earlier show that Syrian influence was still very strong nearly a year after the withdrawal of Syrian troops and secret services from Lebanese territory.

6   In fact, of the 30 countries that operate nuclear reactors, only a third produce their own fuel.

7   Iran owns 13% of global oil and 10% of global gas reserves.

8   Two contracts were signed in February 2005, one for an initial fuel consignment at the beginning of 2006, and the other relating to the supply of subsequent consignments between 2007 and 2017.

9   Military involvement in the Iranian nuclear programme covers *inter alia*: the Gchine mine, centrifuge workshops, uranium casting, polonium 210 and beryllium experiments, high explosive tests plans, nuclear work at the Lavizan facility, redesign of the Shehab 3 nose cone.

10 It must be emphasised that the plan to produce enriched uranium at the Russian-built Natanz facility could not supply the Bushehr reactor in any event, even if Moscow cut off its supplies, unless Moscow gave Iran the technical specifications and codes which is not in its interest to provide.

11 This laser enrichment programme, currently dismantled (at least on this site), received external help from two major sources: Russia and China.

12 The governors of the IAEA have repeatedly asked Tehran to halt construction on this reactor, clearly destined to produce nuclear weapons, without obtaining the slightest result.

13 The documents that led to this decision were repeatedly requested from Tehran by the international inspectors, in vain.

14 This is the nuclear network whose numerous misdemeanours were dis-
    closed in December 2003, when Colonel Gadaffi announced that he had
    decided to terminate his non-conventional weapons programmes.

15 Iran organised a team as early as 1974 to develop a laser system and told
    the IAEA in August 2003 that experiments in this area had been discon-
    tinued. However, a Russian engineer told *Der Spiegel* in summer 2006
    that since 2004 Iran has sought and secured technical aid from Russia for
    its laser system which may have moved to the Parchin military complex.

16 That is the reason why the IAEA took specific control measures when a
    reactor of this type was discovered in Algeria in the early 1990s.

17 The "pledges" made by North Korea on 19 September 2005, which aroused
    fresh hopes since they involved abandoning the development of any kind of
    nuclear weapons, were of course broken, and we find ourselves in 2006 in
    a situation where diplomacy has not made any headway.

18 Tehran did not agree to the precondition that it halt enrichment and re-
    processing related activities before the resumption of talks.

19 As a matter of fact, the offer reportedly led to a secret technical coopera-
    tion agreement covering military and nuclear deals.

20 The package comprised P1 designs, 500 components for P1 machines,
    and drawings for the more advanced P2 centrifuge.

21 The Iranians claim that this is due to the "secret nature" of the Iranian
    regime at the time when the transaction took place.

22 Documents were handed over to the IAEA with great reluctance in Feb-
    ruary 2005. The Vienna Agency openly questioned whether these docu-
    ments were comprehensive. Then, in November 2005, it was discovered
    that the inspectors in Iran had been granted access to other information
    concerning technologies directly related to producing the bomb.

23 For example, Iran approached China, Russia, Germany, Kazakhstan and
    the UK in an attempt to obtain beryllium, used for making nuclear weap-
    ons, according to experts.

24 The chief Iranian negotiator under President Khatami. He filed a report
    of his activities after the elections. He was replaced by Ali Larijani.

25 In March 2006, when information on the excavation in Iran of tunnels
    that could house a nuclear explosion was made public, the question could
    have been turned around: would North Korea benefit from an Iranian
    test, in appreciation of its help?

[26] On 5 December 2004, Sirus Nasseri in an interview on the Paris Agreement by Kambiz Tavana for the newspaper *Sharg,* declared that the Iranian authorities had realised "they needed to gain time so as to complete certain projects unimpeded".

[27] Iran has enough components to build about 5,000 centrifuges, but many are not expected to pass quality control. The IAEA considers that Iran has the ability to build 2,000 centrifuges, but the Iranian negotiators continually make reference to 3,000 centrifuges. Nobody can guarantee that the potential number available on Iranian soil is not higher. As a matter of fact, the production of centrifuge components is no longer under IAEA safeguards since February 2006. Rumours of a clandestine plant resurface regularly.

[28] In fact, in January 2006, when Tehran announced it was going to resume uranium enrichment at Natanz, a minimal quantity of 80 tonnes of UF_6 must have been available given the various programmes at Isfahan and the quantities of uranium concentrate introduced into the conversion process.

[29] On 22 August 2006, Iran announced "a very significant achievement" in an undisclosed area.

[30] *Le Figaro* of 5 April 2005, interview with President Khatami.

[31] This is one of the reasons for Mahmoud Ahmadinejad's inflammatory outbursts against the State of Israel in autumn 2005.

[32] Conversely, in January 2006, Cairo voted to submit the Iranian case to the Security Council for information.

[33] The IAEA inspectors initially arranged to carry out inspections in Iran in October 2002, but Tehran constantly postponed the date and finally it was only in February 2003 that the Director General of the IAEA travelled to Iran. The first team of inspectors was not able to operate until 10 March, i.e. seven months after the revelations of summer 2002.

[34] In February 2003, the IAEA learned that Iran intended to build 50,000 centrifuges at Natanz and a heavy-water production plant at Arak. Tehran also admitted having imported from China, in 1991, 2 tonnes of natural uranium in different forms (undeclared). Inspectors were only given access to the Kalaye Electric plant (in Tehran) in summer 2003, after it had been stripped of its contents, then repainted and the floor re-tiled to prevent the inspectors from taking samples that would prove enrichment activities had taken place at this site. Even so, particles of low-

enriched and high-enriched uranium were found there. In May 2003, the Lashkar Abad site where laser enrichment activities had taken place was discovered, but it was not inspected until August 2003. And it was in October 2003 that Iran admitted to having carried out such activities between 1991 and 2000.

[35] Iran's entire strategy clearly consisted of gaining as much time as possible, by arguing either with the Europeans, or the Russians, the Chinese or anybody else.

[36] On 2 November 2003, Ayatollah Khamenei spoke of the Europeans' "excessive demands".

[37] One of the best demonstrations of this unity is the letter from the three European capitals sent on 10 March to the President of the Commission, stating clearly that if the complete suspension of the activities stipulated in the Agreement of 15 November 2004 was not adhered to, they were prepared to go before the Security Council.

[38] In June 2004, when the Iranians resumed some of the activities they had agreed to suspend on 21 October 2003, they declared that the Europeans had not kept their promise to withdraw the question from the agenda of the IAEA's Board of Governors meeting. Needless to say, this promise had never been made.

[39] In fact, this was one of the main points in the preparations, at the end of January 2005, for President Bush's visit to Brussels which took place in February.

[40] And so in March 2005, Washington withdrew its opposition to Iran's entry into the World Trade Organisation and announced it was prepared to consider exporting the parts necessary for Iran's civil aviation programme, which had been hindered by the American embargo.

[41] One of the most worrying aspects of this interview is the statement that: "If we want to make a comparison in technical and legal aspects between our conditions at the present time and at the beginning of the crisis, I think no one can deny that we have made very significant progress since then. From a technical standpoint, the day we started this process, there was no such thing as the Isfahan project. But as of today, we have prepared and tested the Isfahan facility on an industrial level and produced a few tonnes of UF_6. Today, we have a considerable number of completed and ready to use centrifuges. On the surface, it may seem that it has been a year and nine months since we accepted the suspension. But the fact of

the matter is that we have fixed many of the flaws in our work during this period."

[42] On August 21, 2006, Mohammed Saedi, Deputy Director for International Affairs of the Atomic Energy Organization of Iran (AEOI) typically declared that the nuclear programme was now unstoppable.

2. EUROPE: AN INCREASINGLY CONTROVERSIAL STRATEGY

[1] Iran's damage capability in Iraq, Lebanon, Israel and Afghanistan is one of the key elements of the nuclear case, as demonstrated particularly in July 2006.

3. AMERICA: IN A STATE OF PARALYSIS?

[1] In fact, a joint declaration stressed the determination to embark on "a vast defence operation" (7 July 2005). This declaration was followed by the announcement of an agreement on oil and on the construction of three pipelines between Iraq and Iran (18 July 2005).

4. RUSSIA: AN UNRELIABLE PARTNER

[1] Note that the Russian Special Services publicly referred to Iran's nuclear weapons ambitions in 1993, indicating that, without external help, it would take Iran ten years—i.e. until 2003!—to acquire the bomb. In December 1996, the Russian defence minister stated publicly that Iran was "a potential threat to Russia" given its increased "offensive capability".

[2] Iran made it clear to Russia that its role in the region could develop in a negative way.

[3] In fact, two preliminary agreements were signed in August 1992, covering the construction of a nuclear reactor and partnership in the field of nuclear energy for peaceful purposes. This latter part included the supply of research reactors, isotope production, fuel reprocessing and the training of scientists. The 1995 contract for the reactor was worth 800 million dollars, a huge sum for Moscow, particularly at this time and especially as the Iranians had agreed to pay 80% in cash.

[4] The Russians often claim that they have never delivered sensitive nuclear equipment, but that remains open to doubt.

⁵ This agreement, concluded in 1995, was signed before the TNP Review and Extension Conference, which Iran threatened to obstruct. This enabled Moscow, which was very keen to obtain an indefinite extension of this treaty, to threaten Iran with not implementing the agreement.

⁶ Robert J. Einhorn, "A transatlantic strategy on Iran's nuclear program", The Washington Quarterly, autumn 2005.

⁷ The affair was confirmed after the new Ukrainian government arrived in power. In a letter to President Yuchenko in February 2005, a member of parliament condemned this contract referring to an investigation carried out in summer 2004.

⁸ There is still ambiguity over the navigation system of this missile: is it a modern inertial navigation system? In which case, it would be an even more dangerous weapon.

⁹ Declarations by President Putin during his visit to Jerusalem in April 2005. On this occasion, the Russian president indicated that Iran should abandon its fuel cycle project.

¹⁰ Iran's many turnarounds on this issue are listed in the Chronology at the back of this book. Its attitude to the proposal of the five members of the Security Council and Germany in June and July 2006 was very similar and leaves little hope for an acceptable compromise.

¹¹ The fuel contract was signed on 26 February 2005, during a visit to Tehran by Alexander Rumyantsev, head of atomic energy in Russia. Russia is to supply fuel for the Bushehr reactor for ten years, starting in 2006. For a long time, Tehran hesitated to sign this agreement, making all sorts of excuses.

¹² On this point, Moscow's understanding might prove limited, as it will seek to argue that the contract entails a "legal" obligation.

¹³ At a meeting on the Middle East in 2005, a Russian expert revealed that Tehran had asked Moscow to help it "clean up" a site before the arrival of the inspectors (which shows there is still a certain level of trust) which Russia apparently refused to do.

¹⁴ The discussions on the subject that took place between the Europeans and the Russians in Autumn 2005 resulted in failure.

¹⁵ See following chapter.

¹⁶ At the Munich Conference on Security Policy in Europe, in February 2006, the Russian defence minister, Sergei Ivanov, did indeed declare publicly that the Russian proposal stipulated that Iran was not to carry

out any conversion or enrichment activities. But this was not in Russia's written declaration, which did not mention a word about Iran.

[17] In summer 2005, Iran was offered observer status within this group.

[18] In summer 2005, Tehran declared its ambition to build 20 nuclear reactors, which is utterly unrealistic (20 GW, that sounds more like a negotiation ploy—on Iran's part—than a real project), but which would force Russia to accept an opening up of the market.

5. CHINA: A CLOSE ALLY FOR IRAN

[1] Relations between Iran and China were not good before the Islamic revolution of 1979, but close links have since developed. In 2001, at the 30th anniversary of the opening of diplomatic relations between the two countries, much emphasis was placed on the quality of political relations and the development of bilateral trade. In fact, the volume of bilateral trade is around $3.5 billion, ten times the level of a decade ago. In October 2004, the two countries signed an agreement worth a total of $100 billion, by which China committed to buy Iranian oil and gas and help it develop the Yadaravan facility, close to the Iraqi border.

[2] There are currently a hundred or so operation projects underway between Iran and China, many of which have the purpose of improving the country's infrastructure and/or increasing energy production.

[3] To the east, there is North Korea, which serves this same objective.

[4] China also acquired eight of these submarines, which are ultra silent, and therefore formidable.

[5] In fact, the accusations also implicated former members of the Russian armed forces, which Moscow denied. They allegedly acted as brokers between Iran and North Korea and facilitated the transfer onto Russian soil.

[6] FurtherWhat is more, the murder of Kurdish opponents in Vienna in 1989 was reportedly carried out on the orders of Hashemi Rafsanjani, and the new Iranian president led one of the two commandos.

[7] A conflict between Iran and Pakistan was even envisaged in 1998, when Iranian diplomats were killed at Mazar-i-Sharif by the Taliban who were supported by Islamabad. Moreover, Shia Muslims are regularly killed in Pakistan.

[8] It is essentially a matter of continuing to hide anything that might be compromising. Hence connivance that is hard to establish.

6. PAKISTAN: CLANDESTINE SUPPLIER, UNEASY NEIGHBOUR

[1] For Iranian Shia Muslims, the Taliban represented an unacceptable version of Islam.

[2] In 1998, Iran tested its Shehab 3 missile and Pakistan went ahead with nuclear tests. Troop movements were observed on the Iran-Pakistan border, which the Iranian defence minister, Admiral Ali Shamkani, claimed were justified by "the recent developments in the region ". During this same period, Iranian diplomats were assassinated by the Taliban.

[3] See following pages.

[4] These requests were refused.

[5] Consortium specialising in uranium enrichment by ultracentrifuge, whose Dutch plant at Almelo was burgled in the mid-1970s: blueprints for two types of centrifuge were stolen by Dr AQ Khan.

[6] A series of P2 centrifuge blueprints were shown to the experts. Iran confirmed it had not acquired any centrifuge of this type from abroad nor any components, and that everything had been made locally.

[7] 1 March 2005, Vienna, Austria, IAEA Board of Governors (28 February–4 March 2005) Statement to the Board of Governors by Pierre Goldschmidt, IAEA Deputy Director General, Head of the Department of Safeguards

[8] Iran states that the low- and high-enriched uranium particles from Natanz, the Kalaye Electric Company workshop, Farayand and Pars Trash all have the same source of contamination. Some of the emission signatures of the traces of uranium found in Iran could indicate that they are of Pakistani origin, but not all of them. Others could be from equipment of Russian origin, and others from local enrichment activities.

[9] This formulation indicates Pakistan.

[10] February 2005 report by Pierre Goldschmidt, the IAEA's Head of Safeguards. With regard to the various sites where traces of enriched uranium were found, it is possible that Iran transported contaminated equipment to various places to mislead the inspectors. This hypothesis has sometimes been advanced by the IAEA.

[11] See the article from the *Los Angeles Times* of 26 May 2005, "Pakistan is aiding in Iran inquiry", which emphases Pakistan's change of heart with regard to the IAEA.

[12]   Each important meeting on Iran is preceded by a relaxation of Tehran's stance.

[13]   In fact, in answer to a question put to him by *Der Spiegel* on 28 May, asking how Iran could be dissuaded from seeking to obtain a nuclear bomb, President Musharraf replied: "I don't know. They are very keen to acquire this bomb." To which the spokesman for the Iranian foreign ministry, Hamid Reza Asefi, is said to have replied "Mr Musharraf knows better than anyone that the Islamic republic of Iran has no intentions of acquiring the nuclear bomb".

[14]   Pakistan, like India, refuses to allow international inspectors access to most of its nuclear sites, because of its weapons programme.

7. INDIA: ENERGY NEEDS AND RAPPROCHEMENT WITH WASHINGTON

[1]   *The Discovery of India*, Jawaharlal Nehru, Oxford India Paperbacks, 1990, p. 146.

[2]   The Indian Muslim population includes a high proportion of Shias.

[3]   Oil consumption in India doubled between 1987 and 1999.

[4]   This is not guaranteed, given the consequences of this initiative on US non-proliferation policy, in particular with regard to the Nuclear Suppliers Group, hostile to the deal.

[5]   Iran owns nearly half of the world's natural gas reserves.

[6]   India's natural gas demand is 96 million cubic metres a day whereas only 67 million are available. Most Indian reserves are in the state of Gujarat and the Bombay region.

[7]   By June 2005, it was simply a matter of reaching agreement on the price and deliveries.

[8]   Iranian scientists were however present in Indian laboratories for some 30 years and nobody can be certain what they learned during this period.

[9]   In his public declarations, AQ Khan had always maintained that the Pakistani government was unaware of all his activities until Libya's revelations, but it seems that at least three high-ranking military officials—General Aslam Beg (Chief of staff in the late 1980s), General Karamat (same position from 1996 to 1998) and General Musharraf—were in fact informed. As for the Pakistani secret services, their complicity was necessary to

take sensitive equipment connected to Pakistan's nuclear programme out of the country.

10 It was also one of the priorities of the previous Indian government, whose policy is being pursued by the current coalition, but in a more low-key way for reasons of internal politics.

11 See: "Joint Statement between President George W. Bush and Prime Minister Manmohan Singh", 18 July 2005. See also: "India as a New Global Power, an Action Agenda for the United States", Ashley J. Tellis, Carnegie Endowment for International Peace, July 2005.

8. ISRAEL: AN EXISTENTIAL THREAT

1 All the same, criticism is being expressed, especially in the Gulf states.

2 These unacceptable declarations concerning the State of Israel, repeated three times in autumn 2005, were made anew in February 2006. For the fourth time, there were verbal protests, but no action was envisaged.

3 At the first parade which took place in Tehran in the presence of Mahmoud Ahmadinejad, in 2005, the military attachés of the 25 EU countries left the podium when the missiles went past.

4 It should not be forgotten that in their policy towards Tel Aviv, the Russian leaders are mindful of the large number of Russians who have emigrated to Israel. They are often powerful in the host country and have an equally important influence in their country of origin.

5 It is appropriate to point out here that while the successful attack against the Osirak reactor had the desired effect in the short term, it prompted Saddam Hussein to embark on a much more sophisticated clandestine nuclear programme, with considerable financial and human resources.

6 Given the American operations conducted in Iraq however, coordination between Washington and Tel Aviv is crucial.

9. NORTH KOREA: A ROLE MODEL?

1 A group of Iranian experts and Pasdaran officers was purportedly present at the historic first Korean No-Dong test at the Musudan base on 29 May 1993. Until then, the missiles sold by North Korea to Iran (SCUD B and C) had a range of no more than a few hundred miles. In 1993, Iran is reported to have taken delivery of the first batch of missiles. A similar story surfaced in July 2008, when North Korea tested seven missiles on two different sites.

2   This applied particularly in July 2003 to the Changgwang Sinyong Corporation, already implicated in clandestine trafficking with Pakistan.
3   This is an improvement on the SCUD B missile with a 200-mile range, which North Korea acquired from Egypt.
4   This gas was in Pakistani containers.

1. EGYPT: THE OPPORTUNITY TO RETHINK ITS DEFENCE POLICY?

1   Egypt voted for the IAEA resolution to submit the Iranian case to the Security Council for information.
2   It was not only western countries that were distrustful. An article in *The Times of India* of 28 January 2005 maintained that Egypt was shielded from the suspicions of the international community by America's over-indulgence towards both Cairo and Islamabad.

11. SAUDI ARABIA: OPEN RIVALRY IN THE GULF

1   If this was the intention, it failed to achieve its aim, for the agreement that was concluded with the IAEA on 16 June 2005 is not a general safe-guards agreement, on the grounds that Riyadh is engaged in only minimal nuclear activities.
2   The fear of Iran dominating the region returns since the east of the country has a large Shia population. Riyadh has not forgotten that during the war between Iran and Iraq (Saudi Arabia supported Iraq), Tehran stirred up trouble in this region.

12. SOUTH AFRICA: AN AMBIGUOUS PLAYER

1   The clandestine AQ Khan nuclear network included South African citizens.
2   In 1967, a year before the conclusion of the Non-Proliferation Treaty, Mexico wanted to obtain more explicit safeguards on the right to ben-efit from nuclear energy for peaceful purposes stipulated in article 4 of the treaty. It was particularly a matter of clarifying which technologies were concerned. The proposed amendment, seconded by Romania, was rejected.

13. THE IAEA: NO REFERRAL TO THE SECURITY COUNCIL

[1] His mandate was over at the end of June 2005 and he was replaced by Olli Heinonen, a Finn, who is well acquainted with the Iranian dossier.

[2] *Le Figaro* of 30 June 2005: "Un sentiment d'urgence sur le nucléaire iranien" (A sense of urgency concerning Iran's nuclear activities).

[3] According to Pierre Goldschmidt, "much remains to be done".

[4] For example, when one of the most important decisions on this issue was taken by the Board of Directors, in February 2005, when 27 out of the 35 governors had just voted in favour of referring the entire Iranian case to the Security Council, the Director General of the IAEA did not hold any press conferences and his displeasure was evident.

[5] "How to be a nuclear watchdog" *Foreign Policy*, January/February 2005, p.60.

[6] To mention just a few discoveries: the existence of undeclared tunnels near the Isfahan conversion plant, the Pakistani offer of 1987, Pakistan's supplying of centrifuge components similar to those exported to Iran and the revelation of a bulky document in Farsi concerning the nosecone of the missile (this document was perhaps only handed over to the Agency after June 2005).

[7] For example, following revelations by the opposition, Iran deferred an initial inspection from October 2002 to February 2003. Nobody knows what happened during this four-month period, or, more to the point, what might have been covered up. Second example: the postponement of granting the inspectors access to the Kalaye site from February to August 2003. When access was authorised, the building which was suspected of having housed an enrichment pilot had been thoroughly cleaned and re-painted. Third example: the postponement of an inspection of the Lavizan facility from March to April 2004. By the time access was agreed, several buildings had been razed and the earth around them dug out to a depth of several centimetres, making environmental sampling difficult. Fourth example: the difficulties in gaining access to the Parchin site, where there was a partial inspection on 12 January 2005, which turned out to be fruitless in relation to the needs of the investigation.

[8] It concerns notably what is generally called "additional access", which would have given the inspectors a much fuller understanding of the activities carried out on the Parchin site.

[9] Report of 10 November 2003 to the Board of Governors.

[10]   In August 2006, Tehran refused to provide an entry visa to a third inspector, Trevor Howard, an expert on uranium enrichment.

CONCLUSION

[1]   The reaction of the Swiss banks (Crédit Suisse and UBS) at the beginning of 2006 as well as the effects of referring Iran to the Security Council on trade with Tehran should however prompt the Iranian authorities to consider this question.

[2]   Both Russia and China still appeared reluctant on this point in July 2006.

[3]   Hassan Rohani does not care here about the Europeans, who only began to complain once the works were finished.

[4]   Tehran *Keyhan*, 23 July 2005, p.12.

[5]   Here, the memory of the experience in Iraq will no doubt play an important part.

[6]   See the article by Seymour Hersh in the *New Yorker* of 17 January 2005.

CHRONOLOGY

14 August 2002. At a press conference in Washington, Alireza Jafarzadeh, representative of the NCRI (National Council of Resistance of Iran), reveals that Iran is building two secret nuclear sites: Natanz (vast site part of which is underground for the purpose of enriching uranium) and Arak (heavy-water plutonium production plant).

September 2002. The General Conference of the IAEA decides that its Director General, Mohammed ElBaradei, will visit Iran in October 2002 to inspect activities on the two sites. This visit does not take place until February 2003, having been postponed by Tehran. What may have been hidden during those four months is one of the unresolved questions.

February 2003. During the IAEA's visit, Iran admits for the first time to the existence of a uranium enrichment facility which will ultimately house 54,000 centrifuges, and that it imported nuclear materials of Chinese origin in 1991. Some of these materials were converted to uranium metal, which is useless for a civilian nuclear programme but essential for a nuclear weapons programme.

February, May and July-August 2003. The IAEA is refused permission to take samples from a workshop belonging to the Kalaye Electric Company, mentioned by the opposition in exile, and which housed a centrifuge pilot under cover of a watch manufacturing company. When they are finally authorised to take samples (in August 2003), the inspectors find the premises empty and newly painted from top to bottom.

June 2003. The Director General of the IAEA recognises that Iran has failed to meet its obligations in not declaring imported materials or the sites where these materials are being processed. This is a violation of the Safeguards Agreement.

7–11 June 2003. IAEA inspectors find high-enriched uranium particles which are not covered by any of Iran's declarations. Subsequently, samples revealing enriched uranium of various grades are taken from different sites. Iran's explanations vary.

August 2003. The French newspaper *Le Monde* reports that Iran has attempted to procure from France isostatic presses, vacuum melting furnaces and around thirty telemanipulators through the United Arab Emirates. Iran has also gathered information on flash radiography equipment. All this equipment is clearly needed for a weapons programme.

9–12 August 2003. After the discovery of two types of high-enriched uranium at Natanz, the Iranians mention contaminated equipment for the first time, whereas until now they have not admitted purchasing any equipment overseas. It is also during this inspection that activities involving high-power lasers are noted. Iran declares in autumn 2003 that these activities—uneconomical for a civil nuclear energy programme—took place between 1991 and 2000.

12 September 2003. The IAEA Board of Governors' resolution gives Iran an ultimatum (31 October) for authorising unlimited access to the sites, providing full details of its past programme and suspending all uranium enrichment. Thus the IAEA demanded the suspension of these activities well before any agreement between Iran and the Europeans.

September 2003. Iran declares that the demand to suspend uranium enrichment is unacceptable and announces that the Natanz factory has become operational.

21 October 2003. Agreement between Tehran, Paris, London and Berlin. Iran agrees to answer all the IAEA's outstanding questions and clarify remaining gaps, discrepancies or inconsistencies in its previous explanations; to sign the Additional Protocol to the NPT and commence ratification procedures; and to suspend all uranium enrichment and reprocessing activities. The Protocol gives the inspectors the authority to proceed with more intrusive inspections.

2 November 2003. In Tehran, in front of a large gathering of the military and members of the government, Ayatollah Khamenei condemns the "excessive demands" from overseas. This declaration shows Tehran's duplicity from the moment the Agreement was signed.

26 November 2003. The 35 members of the IAEA Board of Governors condemn Iran, but decide not to refer the case to the Security Council which a strict application of the Agreement would require.

January and February 2004. Following Colonel Gaddafi's revelations, investigations into the AQ Khan Pakistani network uncover substantial co-operation between Pakistan and Iran, including the supply of blueprints for centrifuges as yet undeclared by Iran and more sophisticated than those planned at Natanz (so-called P2 machines, which are significantly faster). It is suspected that they are assembled and tested at sites which are not yet open to the inspectors.

February 2004. Agreement between Iran and the Europeans on the scope of the suspension, which has been the subject of proposals and counter-proposals since November 2003.

March 2004. Iran decides to restrict the activities the international inspectors are authorised to carry out and announces that uranium processing activities will be resumed.

March 2004. The IAEA inspectors discover that six buildings have been razed at the Lavizan-Shian site and that the earth has been dug down to a depth of 1 to 2 metres to impede sampling. This is after Tehran has delayed the inspection by several weeks. Iran's explanation is that the Pasdaran-controlled city authorities needed this site to create a park. It is noteworthy that the Mayor of Tehran of March 2004 becomes the President of the Islamic Republic in August 2005.

6 April 2004. Iran and the IAEA agree on a ten-point plan (which were to be ignored, as were the agreements with the Europeans).

15 June 2004. When the IAEA Board of Governors meets, it is stated that the two crucial issues to be resolved are Iran's activities relating to ultracentrifuge equipment—the plans for which have been acquired from Pakistan—and the source of the various grades of enriched uranium found on several sites. A resolution prompted by Europe deplores Iran's lack of timely co-operation, but does not set Iran a deadline for complying with the IAEA's requests. Even so, Iran reacts angrily declaring that it has other options and that the Europeans should not dictate its behaviour. The same day, the Japanese newspaper *Sankei Shimbun* reveals that Iran and North Korea are actively cooperating, and that six Iranian experts have travelled to North Korea to test nuclear detonators.

22 June 2004. A letter addressed to the German, British and French foreign affairs ministers announces Iran's decision to resume centrifuge production and testing from 29 June. The Europeans reply that they are "disappointed" and remind Iran of its obligations. In July 2005, Dr Rohani, Iran's lead negotiator, admits publicly that during the period from June to November 2004, substantial advances in centrifuge technology were made.

29 June 2004. The IAEA receives a letter from Iran supplying a list of seals to be removed.

11 August 2004. Iran tests an optimised version of the Shehab 3 missile.

September 2004. The IAEA Board of Governors reports limited progress on the two main aspects of the investigation. The Resolution notes with concern the resumption of some processing activities and demands their immediate suspension. Furthermore, the Board asks the Director General to submit a full report in November on Iran's past programme and implementation of the suspension. It is clear that on this date referral to the Security Council is envisaged, with the support of the Europeans, but the threat is not formulated explicitly.

October 2004. New initiative by the three European countries, discussed with the United States which is keeping its distance but is not opposed to it. The proposal is presented at the G8 on 15 October.

21 and 27 October 2004. Negotiations between Iran and the Europeans in Vienna, where the IAEA has its headquarters. The Iranians continue to insist on the voluntary and temporary nature of the suspension, contrary to the European demand for an immediate, irreversible, verifiable and indefinite suspension.

31 October 2004. The Iranian parliament approves a bill (of no great consequence) to force the government to resume its uranium enrichment programme.

5 and 6 November 2004. New round of negotiations in Paris, which are described as "difficult" but do make "some headway". In fact, the central question of the suspension of uranium processing activities is not resolved, nor does Iran agree to the removal of quantities of already processed uranium concentrate or to guarantee that these materials will not be diverted from "civil" nuclear energy generation. Nor is it decided to refer Iran to the Security Council if the negotiations founder.

14 November 2004. Europe-Iran Agreement: Iran is to suspend all enrichment and reprocessing activities for the duration of a lengthy negotiation covering three areas: civil co-operation, trade and regional security.

15 November 2004. Publication of the agreement between the Europeans and Iran, known as the Paris Agreement.

17 November 2004. The National Council of Resistance in Iran in exile (NCRI), which helped divulge several aspects of Iran's nuclear programme, declares at a press conference in Paris that Iran is producing enriched uranium at a facility north of Tehran, where equipment was transported after the demolition of buildings at Lavizan-Shian at the beginning of 2004. Biological and chemical weapons activities are also purported to be taking place there. The same day, Farid Soleimani, one of the main members of the group, declares in Vienna that Pakistan sold Iran a blueprint for a bomb in the mid-1990s through the Abdul Qadeer Khan network, and that it also delivered high-enriched uranium in 2001.

22 November 2004. Beginning of IAEA checks to ensure that Iran has suspended enrichment activities as agreed (from 15 November). Nuclear equipment and materials cited in the agreement are put under seals. Iran comes up with a last-minute objection to putting seals on 37 and then 20 centrifuges. It eventually agrees to allow cameras to be installed, which are easier to deceive. The Europeans agree. It emerges later that some conversion operations continued until February 2005, in violation of the agreement.

25–29 November 2004. IAEA Board of Governors meeting which ends with the voting of a resolution which Iran succeeds in having amended to include two references to the voluntary nature of the suspension.

29 November 2004. The Director General of the IAEA points out that, contrary to the claims by Iran, "there is no time limit for the suspension" of Iran's activities.

30 November 2004. Hassan Rohani, Iran's lead negotiator, boasts of a "huge victory" and states that "Iran has not given up nuclear fuel cycle production", that it "will never give it up" and that it "will go ahead with fuel cycle production".

5 December 2004. Interview with Sirus Nasseri on the Paris Agreement of November 2004, in which he declares that the Iranian authorities had realised "that they needed to gain time to see certain projects through unimpeded".

7 December 2004. The United Press International agency reports the words of Professor Asgarkhani in Tehran. According to him, Iran has stepped up its efforts to acquire the bomb after the discovery of an agreement between Pakistan and Saudi Arabia raising concerns over Riyadh's nuclear weapons ambitions. No confirmation of this accusation has been obtained.

13 December 2004. Opening in Brussels of negotiations between Iran and the Europeans at ministerial level on the three aspects of the 15 November 2004 agreement.

12 January 2005. Partial visit to the Parchin facility, on terms laid down by Iran and highly disadvantageous to the inspectors. The IAEA is later to ask, in vain, to revisit the site where missile and explosive related activities have taken place.

28 January 2005. It is revealed that Ukraine sold six modern cruise missiles to Iran in 2001. These are missiles capable of carrying a nuclear warhead.

February 2005. It emerges that Iran has continued its uranium tetrafluoride conversion activities until now, despite its commitments to the Europeans.

February 2005. President Bush's visit to Europe during which there is a rapprochement between the American view and that of the Europeans.

27 February 2005. Signature of the contract between Russia and Iran for Russia to supply enriched uranium to the Bushehr reactor (for ten years, i.e. the reactor's life span).

28 February–4 March 2005: IAEA Board of Governors meeting. In a written report, the IAEA Head of Safeguards states that a Pakistani offer dated 1987 has been uncovered and acknowledged by Iran. The document in the hands of the IAEA is a copy and probably only part of the original document, which the IAEA requests in vain. The full document may include a blueprint for a bomb. Furthermore, the IAEA has not received the explanations requested concerning past activities at the demolished Lavizan site.

1st February 2005. Information on the boring of tunnels near Isfahan. The inspectors believe they are sites for storing nuclear materials.

April 2005. Iran's attempts to acquire sensitive equipment from Europe continue to surface.

24 April 2005. The spokesman for the Iranian ministry of foreign affairs announces to the press that Iran will resume its uranium enrichment activities: "It is not a matter of years, but of months".

11 May 2005. The Iranian negotiators inform the Europeans of their "irrevocable" determination to resume conversion and then enrichment activities.

2 –27 May 2005. Review Conference of the Parties to the Treaty on the Non-Proliferation of Nuclear Weapons. Iran avoids all criticism and even being mentioned.

25 May 2005. Meeting in Geneva of the three European ministers and Javier Solana, Secretary General of the European Union, with the Iranian negotiator Hassan Rohani. The upshot of this meeting is that the Paris Agreement is maintained and the Europeans pledge to submit a proposal to Iran within three months specifying that it will not provide for Iran to develop fuel cycle activities.

24 June 2005. The ultra-conservative Mahmoud Ahmadinejad is elected president of Iran with 61.69% of the votes and a turnout of 59% of registered voters.

29 June 2005. Publication of the American Executive Order on the freezing of assets of companies assisting the proliferation of weapons of mass destruction.

23 July 2005. Hassan Rohani declares that the discussions with the Europeans have made it possible for Iran to gain time and make important progress in key sectors. He also states that the number of operational centrifuges in Iran "is considerable", whereas the IAEA is only aware of 164 assembled centrifuges (the first cascade of the Natanz pilot).

27 July 2005. Tehran announces, a few days before the investiture of the new president, that it will resume its conversion activities, with or without the Europeans' agreement.

31 July 2005. Letter from Hassan Rohani to President Khatami presenting the report on his nuclear actions. In it he announces that Iran is embarking on the last stage of the programme. The production of a sufficient quantity of UF_6 can effectively enable Iran rapidly to produce the fissile materials necessary for a bomb.

1ˢᵗ August 2005. Iran announces its intention of resuming conversion activities at the Isfahan plant and informs the International Atomic Energy Agency verbally of its decision. This verbal note asks the IAEA to take the necessary steps to permit the resumption of activities (i.e. the presence of inspectors for the breaking of the seals placed by the IAEA on the facilities covered by the suspension). The same day, one of the chief negotiators, Hossein Moussavian, declares that "the game is over".

2 August 2005. The three Europeans reply to Hassan Rohani, announcing that the IAEA has called an extraordinary meeting of the Board of Governors in the week of 8 August, to respond to Iran's decision.

3 August 2005. Inaugural address by the Iranian president in which he says that "the imperialists' weapons of mass destruction must be eliminated".

8 August 2005. Iran resumes its uranium conversion activities at Isfahan after the installation of cameras by the IAEA, carried out hastily at Iran's request.

9 August 2005. The IAEA Board of Governors votes by consensus for a weak resolution asking Iran to revert to the suspension of its conversion activities, and setting the date of 3 September for the presentation to the Council of a complete report by the IAEA on the implementation of safeguards. There is no provision for measures to be taken if Iran does not comply.

14 August 2005. Formation of the new Iranian government: confirmation of the ultra-conservative tendency and a reminder of Iran's resolve to pursue its nuclear programme.

24 August 2005. The Iranian parliament rejects four of the ministers proposed by Ahmadinejad, including the oil minister, who worked closely with him when he was Mayor of Tehran.

25 August 2005. Iran's new negotiator, Ali Larijani, declares he wants to open discussions to other players than the three Europeans.

29 August 2005. At the annual conference of French Ambassadors, the French President points out that Iran is in danger of leaving the Europeans no choice but to refer the case to the Security Council.

2 September 2005. IAEA report on the implementation of safeguards in Iran. The document lists all the past violations (non-declaration of nuclear materials imports and processing, non-declaration of nuclear sites, particularly the Kalaye Electric workshop which housed the enrichment pilot, and the Lashkar Abad facility which housed the laser enrichment pilot, non-declaration of tunnels designed to store the products converted at Isfahan, non-declaration of plutonium experiments from 1993, failure to provide satisfactory information concerning the Pakistani offer of 1987, or activities related to P2 centrifuges, the blueprints for which were acquired from Pakistan in 1994-1995.

14–16 September 2005. Summit on the reform of the UN in New York. Speech by President Ahmadinejad reaffirming Iran's right to develop fuel cycle activities and proposing to extend the negotiations to other partners, including China and South Africa.

19 September 2005. Meeting of the IAEA Board of Governors. The Europeans immediately propose a draft resolution asking for Iran to be referred to the Security Council.

20 September 2005. Iran reacts by threatening to withdraw from the NPT and to refuse to sell oil to countries that support the resolution.

22 September 2005. Although the Europeans have the requisite majority for the Board of Governors to refer Iran to the Security Council, they decide to amend the resolution and remove all references to transferring the case.

16 October 2005. President Ahmadinejad declares: "the presence of British troops in southern Iraq and on the Iranian border is causing the Iraqis and the Iranians to feel insecure. We strongly suspect the British troops of terrorist acts."

16 October 2005. Article in the *Sunday Telegraph* revealing a ballistic missile deal between Russia and Iran led by former members of the Russian armed forces, involving the transfer of North Korean technology to Iran.

19 October 2005. Meeting of the Nuclear Suppliers Group (NSG), which discusses the principle of suspending supplies to Iran.

26 October 2005. President Ahmadinejad, at a conference in Tehran on "A world without Zionism", declares that "Israel must be wiped from the map", causing international outrage.

27 October 2005. Iran launches its first satellite, Sinah 1, designed by the Russian firm Polyot.

2 November 2005. Tehran announces that 40 ambassadors and heads of mission will be recalled to Iran in the coming months. These include the Iranian ambassadors to London, Paris, Berlin and Geneva.

2 November 2005. Reuters announces a Russian offer to Iran to produce the necessary fuel for Bushehr jointly in Russia. Enrichment would also be carried out on Russian soil.

25 December 2005. Iran rejects Moscow's proposal to carry out uranium enrichment operations in Russia so as to provide the requisite safeguards for its nuclear programme, stating it will only accept proposals recognising its right to carry out enrichment on its own soil. At the same time, Tehran claims not to have received any concrete proposal from Russia, further to which Russia makes its proposal public to prove its existence.

30 December 2005. Going back to its earlier declaration, Iran announces it is ready to examine the Russian offer, the content of which has not been disclosed, following an intervention by Security Council chief Igor Ivanov.

2 January 2006. Back to square one: in a televised interview, Ali Larijani, Iran's lead negotiator, describes the Russian proposal as "only a few lines long and not well thought out", and that it "had serious flaws".

3 January 2006. Tehran verbally informs the IAEA of its decision to resume enrichment activities.

8 January 2006. The European Union calls on Iran not to resume enrichment activities.

10 January 2006. The five permanent members of the Security Council each address to Tehran via the Iranian ambassador to Vienna a message urging Iran not to resume enrichment activities, to cooperate more fully with the IAEA and to resume serious negotiations. Reply from Ayatollah Khamenei: Iran will never relinquish its nuclear programme and is not afraid of sanctions.

10 January 2006. Iran removes 52 seals on the Natanz, Pars Trash and Farayand sites.

16 January 2006. Agreement of the Five on a two-stage process for referring the case to the Security Council. The first stage will consist only of "informing" the Council.

19 and 20 January 2006. On a visit to Syria, President Ahmadinejad declares: "Our position on regional issues is clear: we reject any foreign interference". These words apply equally to Iran's nuclear programme, the call for Hizbullah to disarm and to the investigation into the murder of former Lebanese prime minister Rafiq

Hariri. He also declares: "Syria and Iran will form a new front against arrogance and domination".

21 January 2006. The Israeli defence minister Shaul Mofaz, declares that "Israel cannot accept an Iranian nuclear capability".

23 January 2006. Satellite images from the Natanz site which appeared on the ISIS site and were published in the *Sunday Telegraph* show new buildings.

23-24 January 2006. Negotiations between Iran and Russia in Moscow. Russia says it is prepared to examine the possibility of China being part of the consortium. A few days later, Ali Larijani is in Beijing, commenting that "the capacity of Russia's proposal does not meet all the nuclear energy needs of Iran".

4 February 2006. The Board of Governors votes by a large majority (27 out of 35 votes) for a resolution asking the IAEA Director General to hand over all the reports and all the resolutions concerning Iran to the Security Council for information. However no action is envisaged before March, when the Director General of the IAEA's report to the Governors is to be made.

8 February 2006: The *Washington Post* reports the discovery of plans for a 400-metre tunnel apparently designed for an underground atomic test. The information is uncorroborated.

27 March 2006: communiqué from the Baha'i religious community of France, divulging a letter from the supreme leader Ali Khamenei to the chief of staff of the Iranian army on 29 October 2005, asking him to enlist the intelligence services, the police and the Revolutionary Guards in taking a census of members of the Baha'i religious minority.

29 March 2006: adoption of a declaration by the President of the Security Council without voting, after several weeks of discussions. This declaration gives Iran 30 days to comply with the demands of the IAEA, set out in the first operative paragraph of the resolution of February 2006. First of all Iran must "reinstate the complete and permanent suspension of all enrichment and reprocessing activities, including research and development activities". Iran's response is immediate: its envoy to the IAEA, Ali Asghar Soltanieh, tells Vienna that "Iran's decision on enrichment is irrevocable, particularly in the fields of research and development".

30 March 2006: Foreign minister Manouchehr Mottaki, on a visit to Geneva, declares that referral to the Security Council is "totally unacceptable and inappropriate".

31 March to 5 April 2006: Iranian military manoeuvres (code-named "Great Prophet") in the Strait of Hormuz where various torpedo and missile tests are carried out. The leader of the Revolutionary Guards, General Yahia Safavi, declares on 4 April that Iran can use this strategic area, through which nearly 20% of global oil output passes, to exert pressure on the foreign powers. He also calls for the withdrawal of America's 5th fleet, stationed in Bahrain.

2 April 2006: Iran's envoy to the IAEA, Ali Asghar Soltanieh, unaware of the Security Council's demands of 29 March, declares: "The best thing the Security Council can do is to take note of the documents submitted to it and allow the IAEA to do its job".

9-10 April 2006: press articles in the *New Yorker* (Seymour Hersh) and the *Washington Post* on preparations for military operations against Iran prompt the US president to point out that "the doctrine of prevention is to work together to prevent the Iranians from having a nuclear weapon. ... It doesn't mean force necessarily. In this case, it means diplomacy". Consistent with America's usual position, nothing is ruled out, even if diplomacy is the preferred option.

10 April 2006: Javier Solana declares that the European Union "should begin to envisage the possibility of sanctions against Iran".

11 April 2006: Gholam Reza Aghazadeh, Iran's Vice president and director of the Iranian Atomic Energy Organisation (IAEO), announces, in the presence of President Ahmadinejad, that on 9 April, Iran succeeded in enriching uranium to 3.5%. He adds that Iran's ambition is to assemble 3,000 centrifuges by the end of 2006. The Iranian president announces that Iran has joined "the group of countries that have nuclear technology". Most capitals deem this announcement, which defies the demands of the IAEA and the Security Council, significant.

13 April 2006: the Director General of the IAEA visits Tehran, under difficult conditions given the announcement made two days earlier. This visit does not result in any public communication, but is generally interpreted as a failure.

18 April 2006: meeting in Moscow of the political directors of the five permanent members of the Security Council and of Germany. No agreement is reached on the issue of sanctions.

19 April 2006: in an interview published in the Egyptian newspaper *Al Ahram*, President Chirac of France states that "the prospect of an Iran with a nuclear bomb is unacceptable", adding that "Iran is (also) pursuing a missile programme that is causing concern".

25 April 2006: During the visit by the President of Sudan Omar al-Bashir, the supreme leader Ali Khamenei declares that Iran is ready to transfer its experience and its nuclear technology to other countries.

28 April 2006: the report to the Director General of the IAEA states that Iran has not implemented any of the measures requested by the Security Council, and that in two areas at least (P2 centrifuges and plutonium) the situation has deteriorated even further.

2 May 2006: meeting of the political directors of the five permanent members of the Security Council and of Germany. Despite the IAEA's very negative report and Russia's declarations that enrichment is a "red line", the situation has still not evolved with regard to Chapter 7 and sanctions.

29 May 2006: in an interview by *Der Spiegel*, Mahmoud Ahmadinejad demands the setting up of an "independent" research team to investigate the Holocaust. The interview triggers outrage in the German press.

29 May 2006: plenary meeting of the Nuclear Suppliers Group in Brasilia. The European Union presents a programme for reinforcing the existing control mechanisms for exports to Iran. France notably produces an additional list of materials that have a dual use; marked reticence on the part of China.

31 May 2006: American Secretary of State Condoleezza Rice announces in Washington that the USA is prepared to take part in resumed negotiations with Iran if Tehran suspends all enrichment and reprocessing activities, as requested by the Board of Governors and the Security Council. It is the first time since 1979 that Washington agrees to enter into direct discussions with Tehran.

1st June 2006: the five permanent members of the Security Council, Germany and the European Union reach an agreement in Vienna on a new offer to Iran and on the prospect of new Security Council measures if Iran refuses it. Iran has three weeks to respond to the proposal.

6 June 2006: the offer is presented to Tehran by Javier Solana. Tehran's initial reaction, conveyed by Ali Larijani, is not entirely negative. But the very same day, activities resume at both Isfahan and Natanz, signalling that Iran refuses to suspend its conversion and reprocessing activities, as Ayatollah Khamenei stated a few days earlier.

12 June 2006: report from the Director of the IAEA to the Board of Governors. No progress is reported on the pending issues: particularly concerning high- and low-enriched uranium contamination and information on the P2 centrifuges. Furthermore, the report confirms that a new conversion campaign has begun at Isfahan, and that UF_6 has been introduced into the first 164-centrifuge cascade at Natanz. Finally, the IAEA has found traces of high-enriched uranium on the military site of Lavizan which was partially demolished in 2004.

20 June 2006: on the fringes of the meeting of the Organisation of the Islamic Conference (OIC) in Baku (Azerbaijan), Iran's foreign minister, Manouchehr Mottaki, declares that he is not in a position to say when Iran will have finished formulating its response (expected by the Six on 23 June).

21 June 2006: Iran's President Mahmoud Ahmadinejad declares in a televised speech that Iran "will examine" the offer "and, if it is God's will, we will submit our opinion by the end of the month of Mordad" (which ends on 22 August). Iran therefore will not meet the deadline of 23 June. This new deadline is not accepted by the Six.

11 July 2006: Meeting in Brussels between Javier Solana and an Iranian delegation led by Ali Larijani. The High Representative for the Common Foreign and Security Policy (CFSP), is expecting a response from them to the proposal of 6 June. This is not forthcoming and the meeting ends in complete deadlock.

12 July 2006: The foreign affairs ministers of the permanent five members of the Security Council and of Germany meeting in Paris issue a joint declaration in which they decide to refer Iran to the Security Council to make suspension compulsory.

12 July 2006: A Hizbullah raid on the Israel-Lebanon border kills eight Israeli soldiers and kidnaps two others, triggering a large-scale regional crisis. This raid is interpreted by many observers as a diversion tactic instigated by Iran with the help of Hizbullah, just as the Iranian case was handed over to the Security Council.

19 July 2006: The Security Council begins to study a resolution curbing Iran.

20 July 2006: Ali Larijani declares that some of the fuel required for Bushehr will be produced in Iran, thus affirming once again Iran's refusal to comply with the demands of the Security Council.

28 July 2006: Security Council discussions of the draft resolution are postponed.

28 July 2006: US sanctions on a number of foreign companies, including Rosoboroexport and Sukhoi in Russia. Moscow protests.

30 July 2006: Hugo Chávez, president of Venezuela, makes an official visit to Tehran, where he is called "brother of the whole Iranian nation" by Mahmoud Ahmadinejad.

31 July 2006: UN Resolution 1696 is adopted with 14 votes in favour and one against (Qatar). Suspension of all enrichment and reprocessing related activities is now mandatory. Iran has one month to comply. Further measures could be adopted in the event that Iran rejects the resolution. Rejection comes one day later and is repeated by different actors, including Ali Larijani, in the following days.

6 August 2006: According to *The Sunday Times*, Iran allegedly tried to import large quantities of uranium from Congo in October 2005. It is worth noting that Iranian uranium deposits contain elements of molybdenum, which contaminate hexafluoride (UF_6) if they are not removed.

22 August 2006: The Iranian government does not accept the condition set by the 6 nations for talks, but propose negotiations in a written document that is not made public. The 1696 UNSC resolution giving Iran 30 days to stop the programme has been ignored.

BIBLIOGRAPHY

AFP, "Iran's Rafsanjani Warns Israel against Attacking Nuclear Sites", September 18, 2003.

AFP, "Nuclear Armed Iran Would Be More Vulnerable", 9 June 2004.

Associated Press, "Pakistan knew of Nuclear Black Market", 7 March 2004.

Agazadeh, Reza, "Official says world surprised by Iran's nuclear technology" Mehr News Agency, Tehran, 10 December 2004.

Albright, David and Corey Hinderstain, "Iran, Player or Rogue?" *Bulletin of Atomic Scientists*, vol. 59, no. 5, September October 2003.

Bron, Schlomo, *Middle East Military Balance*, Tel Aviv: The Jaffe Center for Strategic Studies, 2005.

Brzezinski, Zbigniew and Brent Scowcroft, *Iran: Time for a New Approach*, Council on Foreign Relations, July 2004.

"The China-Iran Nuclear Cloud", Mednews, July 22, 1991.

Chubin, Sharham, "Iran's Strategic Predicament", *The Middle East Journal*, vol. 54, no. 1, 2000.

——, *Whither Iran? Reform, Domestic Politics and National Security*. Adelphi Paper 342, London: Oxford University Press, 2002.

Chubin, Sharham and Charles Tripp, *Iran-Saudi Arabia Relations and Regional Order*. Adelphi Paper 304, London: Oxford University Press, 1996.

Delpech, Thérèse, "Trois Européens à Téhéran", *Politique Internationale*, no. 106, Winter 2004-2005.

——, "Trois Européens à Téhéran, Suite et Fin", *Politique Internationale*, no. 108, Summer 2005.

——, "L'Iran et la Bombe: Options de Fin de Partie", *Politique Internationale*, no. 111, Spring 2006.

141

———, "L'Iran Nucléaire: la Course contre la Montre", *Politique Etrangère*, September 2005.

———, "Iran 2006, pessimisme sans limites", *Commentaire*, September 2006.

Einhorn, Robert, "A Transatlantic Strategy on Iran's Nuclear Programme", *The Washington Quarterly*, vol. 27, no. 4, Autumn 2004, p.28.

Eisenstadt, Michael, *Turkish-Israeli Military Co-operation. An Assessment*, Policy-Watch 262, Washington Institute for Near East Policy, July 24, 1997.

Everts, Steven, *The EU and Iran: How to Make Conditional Engagement Work*, Policy Brief, Centre for European Reform.

Fizpatrick, Mark, "Iran and North Korea: the Proliferation Nexus," *Survival*, vol. 48, no. 1, Spring 2006, p.61.

Gulf News, "No Impediments for Iran To Build Centrifuges", July 15, 2004.

Henderson, Simon, *Toward a Saudi Nuclear Option: The Saudi Pakistani Summit*, Policy Watch, no. 793. The Washington Institute for Near East Policy, October 2003.

Howard, Roger, *Iran in Crisis: Nuclear Ambitions and the American Response*, London: Zed Books, 2004.

Human Rights Watch, *Iran, 2004*.

International Institute for Strategic Studies, *Iran's Strategic Weapons Programmes: a Net Assessment*, Abingdon: Routledge for the IISS, 2005.

Jack, Andrew, Stephen Fidler and Roula Kalaf, "Russia in Talks to build Syrian Nuclear Reactor", *Financial Times*, 16 January 2003.

Katzman, Kenneth, *Iran: US policies and Options*, Congressional Research Service Report for Congress, 14 January 2000.

Kemp, Geoffrey, *Iran's Nuclear Weapons Options: Issues and Analysis*, Nixon Center 2001, Washington DC.

Kessler, Glenn and Dana Linzer, "Nuclear Evidence could point to Pakistan." *Washington Post*, 3 February 2005.

Larijani, Ali, "Now is the time for Resistance", Farhang-e Ashti website, 30 November 2005.

Larrabee, Stephen and Ian Lesser, *Turkish Foreign Policy in an Age of Uncertainty*, Centre for Middle East Public Policy, National Security Research Division, Rand, 2003.

Nasr, Vali and Ali Gheissari, "Foxes in Iran's Henhouse," *The New York Times*, 13 December, 2004.

Pollack, Kenneth, *The Persian Puzzle: The Conflict between Iran and America*, New York: Random House, 2004.

Rowhani, Hassan, "Iran needs to counter multi dimensional threats from the West", IRNA website, 14 January 2006.

Russel, Richard L., "A Saudi Nuclear Option?" *Survival*, vol. 43, no. 2, Summer 2001.

Sanger, David, "In face of report, Iran acknowledges buying nuclear components", *The New York Times*, 23 February, 2004.

———— and William Broad, "Iran admits that it has plans for a newer centrifuge", *The New York Times*, 13 February, 2004

Scowcroft, Brent, "An opening to Iran", *The Washington Post*, May 11, 2001.

Sick, Gary, *America's Fateful Encounter with Iran*, London: I.B. Tauris, 1985.

Schake, Kori N. and Judith S. Yaphe, "The Implications of a Nuclear-Armed Iran", *McNair Paper* 64, Washington, DC: National Defense University, 2001

Sneh, Ephraim and Graham Allison, *Nuclear Dangers in the Middle East: Threats and Responses*, Washington Institute for Near East Studies, May 2005.

Sokolski, Henry, "That Iranian nuclear headache", *National Review Online*, 22 January, 2004.

Takeh, Ray, "Iran Builds the Bomb", *Survival*, vol. 46, no. 4, Winter 2004-2005.

Vick, Karl, "Iran Asserts Right to Nuclear Weapons", *Washington Post*, 11 March, 2003.

Walker, William, *Weapons of Mass Destruction and International Order*, Adelphi Paper 370, London: Oxford University Press, 2004.

Warner, Tom, "Ukraine sold Cruise Missiles to Iran, China", *Financial Times*, 3 February, 2005.

FURTHER READING AND USEFUL LINKS.

Implementation of the NPT Safeguards Agreement in the Islamic Republic of Iran. Reports by the Director General of the IAEA dated 10 November 2003, 15 November 2004, 18 November 2005 and 27 February 2006. http://www.iaea.org/Publications/Documents/Board/2003/gov2003-75.pdf; http://www.iaea.org/Publications/Documents/Board/2004/gov2004-83.pdf; http://www.iaea.org/Publications/

Documents/Board/2005/gov2005-87.pdf; http://www.iaea.org/Publications/Documents/Board/2006/gov2006-15.pdf

Resolutions adopted by the IAEA Board of Governors on 11 August 2005, 24 September 2005, 4 February 2006, http://www.iaea.org/Publications/Documents/Board/2005/gov2005-64.pdf; http://www.iaea.org/Publications/Documents/Board/2005/gov2005-77.pdf; http://www.iaea.org/Publications/Documents/Board/2006/gov2006-14.pdf

The offer of the Six (USA, China, Russia, United Kingdom, France, and Germany) of summer 2006; http://www.iaea.org/Publications/Documents/Infcircs/2006/infcirc676.pdf

UN Security Council presidential declaration of 29 March 2006; http://daccessdds.un.org/doc/UNDOC/GEN/N06/290/89/PDF/N0629089.pdf? OpenElement

UN Security Council Resolution 1696 of 31 July 2006; http://www.un.org/News/Press/docs/2006/sc8792.doc.html

INDEX

DEMCO